the ultimate success mindset

Vince Gabriele

CONTENTS

INTRODUCTION

Several years ago, I was given a book that changed my life.

I read a book called *Mindset: The New Psychology of Success* by Carol Dweck that changed the way I think about everything.

When I saw the positive impact it had on myself I needed to let people know about this belief system, a belief system that helped me succeed in every aspect of my life.

It helped me become a better husband, a better father. It helped me as an entrepreneur, as a business coach, a leader, and as a friend.

I have accumulated wealth from this mindset beyond my dreams physically, mentally, financially, and emotionally.

I decided to write about it, every week, for three years. This book is a collection of the articles I wrote. Every week I got the opportunity to help someone get through their day better, to get them through a difficult time in their life, to think differently about their failures, to realize their true potential.

I got the opportunity to help people realize that their failures don't define them. Instead, their failures are the gateway to greater success if they think about them in a productive way.

I hope you get the same result from this book.

ACKNOWLEDGEMENTS

Vanessa, Bella, Toria, and Joey

Marlene and Joseph Gabriele

Ang, Jess, Ash(Dino)

G-UNIT

PVK, Max, Remi, and Liv

Christus Family

Schleimer Family

GG and Clayton

Mike Waldron

The GFP Team: Tom, Joe, Bern, Chris, Gina, Michelle, Megan, Ellers, Messy Matt,

Paul Reddick

John Haddad

Dr. Rob Gilbert

New Providence Football

Temple Football

In Memory of Carl Demilio, our great friend who always had the Growth Mindset

CHAPTER 1: GETTING A GROWTH MINDSET

The greatest of all human freedom is the ability to respond to any given circumstance. We retain our freedom to choose our attitude and actions in response to whatever life deals us.

— *Victor Frankel*

I have good news for you—you have the Growth Mindset inside of you.

I know this because you were born with it. We all were. A baby does not have trouble crawling and just quit. It keeps trying until it crawls; it simply keeps going.

Then, when we get older, we get challenged. People criticize us. We fail a test. We get cut from that team. We get fired from our job. We need a tutor. We may be told that we will never be able to do something. You may find that you have a disability.

The one common thing we all hold is our response to all these things: we hold the key for our thoughts.

- We can view criticism as something that diminishes our worth—or as a way to get better from that information.
- We can view that test that we failed as we stink at that subject—or we found out that maybe we did not do all we could to succeed and next time we must prepare harder.
- We can view getting cut from that team as I got robbed—or we can use it as motivation to be so much better the next time that there is no possible way you could get cut again.
- We can view getting fired from a job as I was not worth it for that company to keep me—or figure out how can I

improve so at the next job they will have no choice but to keep paying me more money.

- We can view the need to have a tutor as I am deficient in that subject—or the extra effort I am putting in will pay off for me big time.

- We can believe someone who tells us we can't do something— or we can prove them wrong.

- We can use our disability as an excuse—or as an opportunity to make our strengths even stronger.

You are in control of this. You are the only person that can stop you.

Understand the Fixed Mindset but think with the Growth Mindset, and you will find yourself never worrying about what happened, just how you can learn from it.

What Is the Growth Mindset?

The Growth Mindset is a philosophy I have embraced, and I think it can help everyone grow and become a better person. Babies come with the Growth Mindset, but we lose it as we grow older, as we get ingrained habits and learn to have a Fixed Mindset.

The Growth Mindset person practices:

- Learning from failure
- Viewing challenges as opportunities to learn
- Using obstacles as information for future success
- Seeing the success of others as potential for them

Here's a look at how the Growth Mindset and how it works. First, though, we need to understand the Fixed Mindset.

People who hold these beliefs think that "they are the way they are," but that doesn't mean that they have less of a desire for a positive self-image than anyone else. So of course, they want to perform well and look smart. But to achieve these goals …

By definition, a challenge is hard and success is not assured, so rather than risk failing and negatively impacting their self-image, they will often avoid challenges and stick to what they know they can do well.

Same with obstacles. The difference here, as I see it, is that challenges are things that you can decide to do, while obstacles are external forces that get in your way.

What's the point of working hard and making efforts if afterwards you are still on square one? If your worldview tells you that effort is an unpleasant thing that doesn't really pay dividends, then the smart thing to do is to avoid it as much as possible.

Useful negative feedback is ignored in the best of cases, and taken as an insult the rest of the time. The **Fixed Mindset** logically leads you to believe that any criticism of your capabilities is criticism of *you*. This usually discourages the people around you, and after a while they stop giving any negative feedback, further isolating the person from external influences that could generate some change.

The success of others is seen as a benchmark against which the person looks bad. Usually when others succeed, people with a **Fixed Mindset** will try to convince themselves and the people around them that the success was due to either luck (after all, almost everything is due to luck in the **Fixed Mindset** world) or objectionable actions. In some cases, they will even try to tarnish the success of others by bringing up things that are completely unrelated ("Yes, but did you know about his …").

As a result, they don't reach their full potential and their beliefs feed on themselves: They don't change or improve much with time, if at all, and so to them this confirms that "they are as they are".

Let's now look at the **Growth Mindset**:

People who hold the **Growth Mindset** believe that intelligence can be developed, that the brain is like a muscle that can be trained. This leads to the desire to improve.

And how do you improve? First, you embrace challenges, because you know that you'll come out stronger on the other side.

Similarly, obstacles – external setbacks – do not discourage you. Your self-image is not tied to your success and how you will look to others; failure is an opportunity to learn, and so whatever happens you win.

Effort is seen not as something useless to be avoided but as *necessary* to grow and master useful skills.

Criticism and negative feedback are sources of information. That doesn't mean that all criticism is worth integrating or that nothing is never taken personally, but at least the **Growth Mindset** individual knows that he or she can change and improve, so the negative feedback is not perceived as being directly about them as a person, but rather about their current abilities.

The success of others is seen as a source of inspiration and information. To **Growth Mindset** individuals, success is not seen as a zero-sum game.

And so, **Growth Mindset** individuals will improve and this will create a positive feedback loop that encourages them to keep learning and improving.

Learning

You can't stop the waves, but you can learn to surf."
—Jon Kabat-Zinn

The Growth Mindset teaches us to use every experience in our life as an opportunity to learn.

One of the reasons I read so much is that I am simply fascinated of how much knowledge is out there that I simply have no idea about, knowledge that can make us better people, better at our profession, happier, better parents, better spouses, healthier … you get the picture!

For the first several years of my career, I was focused on becoming the best trainer I could be. I still strive for this, but at this point in my life there are a few other things that are really important for me to become better at. Years ago, I never thought about educating myself to become better.

The first one is being a parent. I feel that some things come naturally based on your own upbringing, but there is so much information out there on how to become the best parent you can be, to raise great kids, and have a happy family.

The Growth Mindset shows I can learn to become a better parent and a better husband.

The message is to be passionate about learning, to become fascinated about all the possibilities that are out there and how there is so much potential to become better at anything.

Challenge yourself to read every day.

Read about happiness, parenting, health, business, struggle, development, nutrition, war, love, success, leadership, time management, energy, motivation, biographies of great people, faith. Just read. There is so much information in this world and ALL of it is at our fingertips.

I recently took a test. The test was designed to help me identify my strengths and talents so I could be aware of them and maximize them in my life. The test was called StrengthsFinder. It is based on five decades of research.

StrengthsFinder identified my number-one strength as Learner. Here is the definition of Learner from the test:

"People who are especially talented in the Learner theme have a great desire to learn and want to continuously improve. In particular, the process of learning, rather than the outcome, excites them."

I was originally confused because I remember hating school pretty much until I started taking exercise science classes in college and decided upon a career as a personal trainer. But after that, my fascination with learning was immense. I could not get enough of it. I went to every seminar, read articles, watched DVDs every night—I was obsessed.

Getting the *Mindset*

A few years ago, I read the book *Mindset: The New Psychology of Success*, by Carol Dweck, and it just hit me hard. This was why I studied and learned so much—I am a learner.

I wanted to practice the Growth Mindset and I wanted to share its power with others. The book fired me up more than any other book I had ever read. It just seemed to make such perfect sense, and now I know why.

My biggest strength or talent is learning.

The purpose of finding your strengths is to maximize them, to refine and sharpen your skills and talents to take advantage of what you love to do the most.

We spend lots of time focusing on our weaknesses. Doing this can be draining, especially if we are dwelling on them and taking no action to improve. On the other hand, discovering your strengths and using them gives you satisfaction, happiness, and accomplishment.

What is your strength?

What is your passion?

Answer this question:

I come alive when … ?

When I Got a Growth Mindset …

I quickly switched my thinking from stressed to learning. I got into a mindset of being excited about the things I messed up because I now had information on how I could make the next time better, no matter what I was doing.

For example, after giving a presentation that I messed up, I sat and wrote down all the things I could do to make the next one better and focused only on improvement instead of focusing on what I messed up on.

While doing this excitement started to build. I was thinking of how great the next one would be once I made these changes. The key to practicing the Growth Mindset is how fast you can go from a Fixed Mindset to a Growth Mindset. In other words, how fast can you go from a state of stress, anxiety, or regret to one of learning, growth, and improvement?

I write about the Growth Mindset every week and I still find myself thinking with a Fixed Mindset. We are not perfect. But …

The faster we recognize a Fixed Mindset and the more aware we are when we think this way, the easier it will be to get to the Growth Mindset. Think about it this way: Your failures and mistakes are opportunities for you to learn and get better.

- Your failures and mistakes are opportunities for you to learn and get better.

- Your failures and mistakes are opportunities for you to learn and get better.
- Your failures and mistakes are opportunities for you to learn and get better.
-

Here is a list of resources I have put together for you to explore this concept further.

Short Article on Mindset

http://mindsetmax.com/mindset/mindsets/growth-mindset/

Official Site of Mindset, Brainology

http://www.mindsetworks.com/default.aspx

2 Minute Clip on Mindset

http://www.youtube.com/watch?v=o8JycfeoVzg

40-Minute Lecture from Carol Dweck, Author of *Mindset*

http://www.youtube.com/watch?v=kXhbtCcmsyQ

My reading journey

"Everything can be taken from a man but one thing: the last of the human freedoms—to choose one's attitude in any given set of circumstances, to choose one's own way."
— Victor Frankel

As I continue on my reading journey, I am realizing how many other books preach the same message as the Growth Mindset.

What I love about the Growth Mindset is that it gives us almost a tangible way to think about every issue in our life. It is a way of thinking that if practiced will bring success.

In his book *The 15 Invaluable Laws of Growth*, John Maxwell discusses the Law of Pain. Specifically, he notes that nobody escapes pain, but few people are able to take negative experiences and turn them into positive ones.

With a Growth Mindset, it is much easier to do this. Here is the formula for turning bad experiences into growth and improvement:

- Embrace that you will have bad experiences.
- Embrace the value of your bad experiences, citing them as the best way to learn.
- Make good changes after bad experiences.
- Take responsibility for your life; you have the opportunity to grow from pain.

Having a growth mindset ...

... doesn't always mean you *won't* fall back into a fixed mindset now and then.

I spent a weekend in Alpena, Michigan, at a Mastermind meeting with a new group I had just joined. The group was small, but I knew everyone in the group was successful, and I was excited for the weekend.

After the first hour, my heart was in my throat. I was not just surrounded by successful people—I was surrounded by people who were more successful than I could have possibly imagined. They were doing things in a day that I did in three, they had focus and drive, and they were all crushing their work every day.

Each person had his own unique success. Some had incredible financial success, some had an unbelievable grasp of their purpose and vision, and many had both.

I found myself very uncomfortable, and I strongly started to doubt that I should even be in this group. I started to have thoughts like, "They will not want to hear anything I have to say," or, "I am a slacker compared to these people."

I had the classic Fixed Mindset.

This thinking strongly hindered my ability to attain the information I needed to help my personal situation and hindered the feedback I was supposed to be providing as a contributing member of the group. I was so focused on being inferior to the others in the group, and I felt that their great success meant that I was not successful.

As someone who is very aware that this is destructive thinking, I was able to recover and get back to Growth Mindset thinking that:

- These people were successful because they earned it
- I needed to use their success as fuel and inspiration
- Their success should excite me because of all the great things I will learn from them

The message here is that we tend to revert to Fixed Mindset thinking when we are uncomfortable or things are hard. We must learn from our experiences, both good and bad, and must push forward.

ME:

ER:

After the weekend, I was excited about what I had learned to help my business, but I was also excited that I had battled away Fixed Mindset thinking and ended up having a very great weekend.

The goal is not to never have the Fixed Mindset—that is inevitable—but rather to be able to find that Growth Mindset as fast as possible.

Back in the day

It was safe to say that when I was in college, I was a weight room warrior. In the college football world, this is NOT a good thing. It usually means you are a stud in the weight room and you suck on the football field. This was me.

I played football in the Big East Conference at Temple University from 1998 to 2001. At the time, we would play teams like Virginia Tech and Miami, both teams were ranked in the top five in the country at that time playing.

I was a very hard worker. I have never been afraid to put my body under extreme stress to become as strong, fast and conditioned as possible. I had the lowest body fat, the best vertical jump, the best squat, and the fastest 40-yard dash among all the lineman. I was consistently in the top 10 on the record board in the weight room for overall performance. None of this mattered much when we got on the field.

My first start as a sophomore came at Byrd Stadium against the University of Maryland. I was to go up against a man named Kris Jenkins, an eventual first-round draft pick and NFL All-Pro.

Nervous was not the word I should use to explain my feelings before this game.

In the first quarter, my body felt paralyzed from being so nervous. I was so tired in the first quarter that I felt as though I had just played two full games. I was the best-conditioned lineman on our team, but all the work I did was thrown out of the window and my mindset quickly turned me into the least-conditioned player on the field.

When you are nervous throughout a game, your body gets very tight. When you play tight, you are slow, you get thrown to the ground easily, and you get exhausted!

Despite all the physical attributes I had worked so hard for, I lacked what I now know to be the Growth Mindset. The Growth Mindset looks at failure as a learning experience and an opportunity to improve. Your self-image is not tied to your success in the Growth Mindset.

The Growth Mindset embraces challenges because you will come out stronger on the other side. In the Growth Mindset, criticism is feedback to help you improve and get better.

I remember thinking on the field, "Oh, man, I am going to get chewed out in the film session tomorrow by my coach." My mindset at the time was a Fixed Mindset. The Fixed Mindset views a challenge as hard, and success as not assured. My Fixed Mindset said, "I am going to look like an idiot in front of 50,000 people so I better not mess up." Fear of making mistakes and looking bad was the reason I played so poorly.

I now live my life with the Growth Mindset. Everything in my life that happens is viewed through the Growth Mindset and I am quick to adjust my attitude if I feel like I am using the Fixed Mindset.

This concept has changed my life, and I am excited to pass on this knowledge to you.

CHAPTER 2: PUTTING IT TO WORK IN THE REAL WORLD

In 2008, I opened Gabriele Fitness and Performance (GFP) in Berkeley Heights, New Jersey. It was a lifelong goal of mine to own my own business, and I am so proud for how far we have come since we opened.

In my time as a business owner, I have learned so much. I have learned about business, training, people, relationships, and team building. There is one lesson that simply makes all of these things work at an accelerated level.

Not too long ago, I read about a very successful business coach talking about the most important thing for success. The most important thing for success, he said, is:

Your ability to adapt to change.

Those who are able to adapt to change will be successful. The ones who resist will fail. There is NO tool, practice, or belief better to adapt to change than the Growth Mindset. In business, things like changes in technology can cause major changes, and the ones who adjust to this are the ones that will come out on top.

We can expect change in our personal lives all the time. When I look back at my life, 20 months ago I had no children. I now have two. If I was not willing to adapt to changes in my life, things would be very difficult.

The Growth Mindset teaches us that it is OK to fail. In fact, failing is the best way learn and improve. Please embrace it and do not be afraid of it.

The Growth Mindset teaches us that is OK for other people to be successful. Many times we are envious or skeptical of this. Instead, we should embrace this and learn from it.

The Growth Mindset sees challenges as opportunities to learn, not a potential to fail.

Other than my family, my business is my greatest joy on earth. I'm grateful to everyone who has helped make it a success, and I'm grateful that I now have a Growth Mindset.

The Growth Mindset gets pink

Not long after our second daughter was born, I spent most of the day painting our new daughter's room pink. I went into it with the best attitude I could, knowing I wanted to do this but also knowing how little experience I have with painting and knowing that I am very poor at these things.

It is funny that I even say that I am poor at painting because I have really only painted a few times in my life. Why would I expect to be good or even know how to paint if I had only done it a few times in my life?

I hear this is the gym all the time. People say, "I am terrible at chin-ups."

I ask, "Well, when was the last time you did chin-ups?"

They typically answer with "Uh … Never."

My response is usually, "Then why would you expect to be good at chin-ups if you have never done them?" They almost always get the picture.

While painting, my good friend John came over to help make sure I had all the right equipment and had a basic understanding of what I needed to do. Finally he left, and I was all alone.

There is a saying—"It is the start that stops most people." This was me.

Before you paint you must take the lid off the paint can. This takes normal people about 30 seconds. Me? Five minutes.

Then I poured the paint into the tray, spilled everywhere. I started painting the lower part of the wall without realizing that my feet were resting on the lid of the paint can and that I was smearing paint all over the floor and my shoes. My mother-in-law was helping, and she was nice enough to clean up after me.

There was a point where I had one crappy corner painted and it looked terrible, I had paint all over myself and the floor, and my wife, Vanessa, just popped in to make sure I knew we had to do two coats tonight.

My blood started to boil. At one point I even started to blame my dad for not teaching me to paint when I was a kid, and then I started to blame Vanessa for not hiring someone to do it.

I was completely stuck in a Fixed Mindset.

I then remembered my Growth Mindset. I remembered thinking, "I am not great at painting because I have hardly ever done it, but

I could be good at it if I had more experience and practice, so this is a necessary step."

I remembered that is NO one's fault except my own and that I must take the responsibility for being such a poor painter.

I thought, this is a project that when done, no matter what it takes, I will be proud of myself.

I changed my attitude, and instead of it being an awful experience, it turned into something I enjoyed because I was learning and improving. We can get better at anything through experience and practice. Our mindset simply needs to reflect this and always be excited about learning and improving. This shines a positive light even the on most frustrating tasks in your life.

The Growth Mindset has truly changed my life. I am better in every area of my life because of it.

An inspiring example: Drew Brees

Drew Brees will go down as one of the best quarterbacks ever. A few years ago, no one would have ever considered him in this category. I was watching him play recently, and I thought to myself, "This guy is so lucky. He just signed a multimillion dollar contract, he's like a rock star in New Orleans, he's a Super Bowl champion, and he's off to the NFL Hall of Fame."

This was NOT luck.

Drew Brees is a self-made superstar due to his Growth Mindset.

He is only six feet tall, several inches below the NFL quarterback average. He was ousted from the San Diego Chargers as the starting quarterback after they drafted Philip Rivers in the first round. He suffered a career-threatening shoulder injury just before he was about to be signed by another team, he was only wanted by two NFL teams, and he choose the New Orleans Saints, at the time an awful franchise, only months after Hurricane Katrina hit and decimated the city.

All odds were against Drew Brees becoming a superstar quarterback in New Orleans.

This guy is the ultimate example of the Growth Mindset.

Many people would have shut down at the thought of their own team drafting another player to replace them. The Fixed Mindset sees this as "you are not good enough," while the Growth Mindset says, "I am going to use this as my fuel and become better." This is exactly what happened to Drew Brees.

Fast forward to six seasons of ultimate success.

The Fixed Mindset says, "Look at all I have accomplished: I have a Super Bowl ring, a new contract, a guaranteed spot in the NFL Hall of Fame. I am good; I can coast through the rest of my career." This happens every year. Players achieve some degree of success and then shut it down.

Drew just keeps getting better every year. He is obsessed with learning and improvement.

When Drew Brees broke Dan Marino's record for most passing yards in a season, his post-game speech was filled with gratitude for coaches, players, equipment managers, athletic trainers, strength coaches, and front office personnel. Never once did he mention himself. It was all about the team and the people who helped along the way.

There are many athletes that we can learn from and I have followed Drew's career closely since he came out of Purdue. This is an athlete that kids should want to be like, not because he is a great quarterback but because of all the other incredible qualities he possesses that make him a champion.

His Growth Mindset, leadership ability, perseverance, discipline with preparation, winning with character, and being one of the most humble professionals in sports makes him a true role model for everyone.

Drew Brees has the Growth Mindset.

Do you practice the Growth Mindset?

The Law of Concentration states that whatever you dwell upon grows and expands in your life. This law says that the more you think about something, the more of your mental capacity is assigned to think about that issue. Eventually, if you are not careful, you will think about it all the time. This law contains a double-edged sword. If you think about something often enough, it eventually dominates your thinking and affects your behavior.

The Law of Concentration and mindset are closely related. Just like concentration, mindset can go either way.

In terms of mindset, we can have the Fixed Mindset, in which we dwell on what is wrong; improvement is not a focus, and most qualities will not get much better.

OR—

We can have the Growth Mindset, in which life is simply one big learning experience with the goal of constant improvement.

If we constantly strive to practice the Growth Mindset, it will expand in our lives, and this way of thinking will be much more present in your life. As I have stated, we must strive to practice the Growth Mindset. We will not always treat every situation with the Growth Mindset, but rather, we must quickly realize that we are thinking with the Fixed Mindset and quickly adapt, That's the key.

I personally still have the Fixed Mindset in many situations in my life. The difference is that I am quickly able to get back to the Growth Mindset.

Here's why:

- Because I wear a bracelet on my wrist that says Growth Mindset
- Because I write about it several times a week
- Because I teach it to others every chance I get
- Because I see the words every time I walk into the weight room
- Because it is one the core values for the GFP team
- Because it is on my top-of-mind awareness
- Because it is a skill I try to improve
- Because I have a lifelong goal of having the Growth Mindset in every situation in my life

The Growth Mindset must be practiced. Like practice in school and sports, you will make mistakes, but you have to realize that your life is like one long practice. It is OK to make a mistake, but you must learn and improve every day from your mistakes.

Teaching your kids about the Growth Mindset

When you talk to your kids about having a Growth Mindset, use words they'll understand.

What is having a Fixed Mindset? It means believing that you have only a certain amount of something, like you can only be so smart or have just so much athletic ability or talent. And that's that.

A Fixed Mindset limits you because it causes you to worry, "I look dumb," or "I look slow." This causes us to not want to take on challenges and we will not learn nearly as much as if we had a Growth Mindset.

On the other hand, having a Growth Mindset is maintaining a belief that things like intelligence, talent, or athletic ability can be developed through their effort, perseverance, strategy, and help from others. Having a growth mindset lets us take on more challenges. We don't worry about things like "I look dumb," or "I look slow." We know we can get more of that ability and accomplish more in the long run.

It's important to instill a Growth Mindset in our kids. But it's just as important to speak to them with a Growth Mindset, especially when we are giving them feedback. Research has proven that when kids are praised for their effort and hard work instead of their athletic ability or intelligence, they welcome more challenges, develop more perseverance, and in turn are more successful.

When a kid comes home with an A on a test, the Growth Mindset way to respond is, "Great job! I am sure you are proud of the effort you put in to achieve that grade."

If a kid scores four touchdowns, say, "I am proud of you! The hard work you put in during practice really made a big difference."

The Growth Mindset rewards kids (and grown-ups!) for improvement, effort, and the hard work of the process, not the result. When a kid comes home with a bad score or had a bad game, the conversation should shift to what they can do to improve the next time or what new strategy could they use to get better.

Focus on improvement, not the result.

Mindset in review

Before we look in detail at how to explore our failures, let's review what we've learned about the Growth Mindset.

The Growth Mindset is thinking and believing that your talent, ability, and intelligence can all be improved through effort. Everything that happens to you is an opportunity to learn and grow. Criticism is taken as information, not a personal attack.

The Fixed Mindset is thinking that you are as you are. Increased effort will yield little improvement. More time is spent focusing on documenting what you have done instead of developing it. Almost all criticism is taken personally.

The best thing about the Growth Mindset is we have complete control over it. You control the mindset you choose to display in every situation. Developing the Growth Mindset takes practice. It is a skill. It is a way of thinking. You will not all of a sudden treat every situation with the Growth Mindset, but please strive to do so.

There will be times where you will catch yourself and say, "That is Fixed Mindset thinking." The more aware you are of this, the better chance you have to be on the Growth Mindset road all the time.

Think Growth Mindset!

CHAPTER 3: LEARNING FROM FAILURE

Your failures picked YOU for a reason.

Looking back at the things I've struggled with in my life, I can always remember the feelings of failure and deficiency I felt at the time. I always struggled in school and labeled myself as academically challenged. I went through a college recruiting process that left me questioning whether I was good enough to play college football. I went through a college football career injured most of the time. I have had major problems in my marriage. As an entrepreneur, there have been times where my health took a back seat and stress was taking over.

At the time of all these challenges, it was very hard to see anything good come out of them. The pain was blinding. It was not until I found myself in a situation to help others with these same exact issues, that I saw the value of these life experiences. At some point, I've had family members, friends, clients, and parents all come to me for help with one of these problems.

And every time I was armed with the life experience to help them.

I was prepared.

As much as it was sometimes painful to rekindle some of these major problems, my pain was not as present as the pain my friends were going through at that time. My new role was the helper, the fixer, the rock. The person that had been in their shoes.

This is a special role.

This is a role that people will remember you forever.

Your failures picked you. They picked you to be able to help others when they go through the same thing. Your failures picked you so YOU can be the rock.

Embrace your struggles, whatever they may be, appreciate them, learn from them.

They are battle armor when others come to you to help them fight.

Making a strong comeback

We all go through times in our lives when things do not work out. The big deal at work falls through, you gain a few pounds, you failed a test, or lost a big game.

These things happen to all of us. Even the most successful people in the world have failed many times.

How we feel about hard times is a mindset. If we focus and think about all the bad things going on in our lives, that is exactly how we will feel. Think about when a kid brings home a report card and has all A's and one C. The focus is usually on the C. What about all the hard work that went into getting the A's? I am not saying C's should be accepted, but recognizing the work that went into the A's is key to shaping the Growth Mindset.

Our thoughts can either be on our problems or how we are going to bounce back from them. If you have a bad meal, you are only one good meal away from being back on track. If you mess up on a test, you must focus your thoughts on how you can score better on the next one, not that you are a failure. If your team loses a game because of your error, it is normal to feel terrible, but letting that feeling move on with you over the course of the next few games will not be productive to you or your team. If you get fired from your job, your family needs you to have the right mindset so you can get back on track.

The quicker we can bounce back and get rid of the negative thoughts, the better off we will be.

We have the power to control our mindset. Your mindset is a choice.

You can choose to dwell on your problems and mistakes, or you can chalk it up to another great learning experience, a way to get better and move on!

My favorite example for this is babies. Unless there is a major problem, all babies eventually walk. They try and try in the beginning and are unsuccessful.

Have you ever heard of a baby that just gave up? As a parent, would you let someone tell your infant to stop trying to walk because they tried many times and were unsuccessful?

We can all learn great lessons from babies.

I've failed—and I'm still failing

Let me tell you a little bit about my failures.

I struggled with weight for many years. Growing up I was always the biggest kid in school. It was cool at some points but many times I felt very different from everyone else.

When I was in sixth grade, I tried to play football. I was about 155 pounds, and the weight limit to play was 140 pounds. It was embarrassing that I had to lose weight as a sixth grader to play on the eighth-grade team.

I started running. Getting around the block was hard. Riding my bike up Maple Street in New Providence was very hard. I could never complete the hill. I always ended up walking up the hill.

I even had to start eating differently. Back then the diet was simply to eat just a little bit. I was used to eating a lot—hence being a 155-pound sixth grader! I eventually made the weight and was on the team.

I had never played football before and every kid on the team was at least two years older than me. I was clearly the worst player on the team. I was a liability, but the rules back then were that everyone had to play six plays every game. When I would get in the game, I would simply protect myself. The chances of me actually making a play were close to impossible because I was so scared.

I remember that one team we played was very good. The coach wanted to put me in for my minimum number of plays, but I begged him not to. He threw me on the field and I got blasted, I think I actually left the ground.

I wanted to quit so bad. I begged my parents to let me quit. I hated football. I was so bad.

But they didn't let me. I reluctantly played the next year and did not have much more success. In eighth grade, something clicked when I made my first tackle. Two years of football, and I had never made a tackle. …

… Four years later, I signed a letter of intent to receive a full scholarship to Temple University to play football. I learned so much from those first two years. I learned so much because I was the worst player on the team and it was really hard. I learned how to stick it out and just get a little better every day.

It was a tough road, though

One of the most difficult times in my life was my senior year of high school. I was being recruited to play football in college, and there was a time where several schools showed a very strong interest in my playing for their team. It was an exciting time. Tons of phone calls, visits during school, and multiple letters every day from college coaches all over the country.

Then it all stopped. I had injured my knee in the beginning of my senior year and ended up having a poor senior football season.

Everything stopped. No more phone calls, visits, or letters. It was as if I had dropped off the face of the earth. It was a very empty feeling, empty because I had linked my happiness in life with something that was really out of my control.

Sure, I had control over how hard I worked, but there are many other factors that go into these decisions. It's similar to a kid wanting to go to an Ivy League school like Harvard or Yale. These kids link their happiness and self-worth on chance and on a few people in admissions. If they do not get in to these specific schools, they are unhappy or feel they are not good enough.

I had this mindset.

I believed since these schools stopped having interest in me that I was a bad football player. I believed since it was looking like I was not getting a scholarship that I had failed. I believed all the hard work I did was for nothing.

I had set a goal for myself of getting a Division I scholarship. When I look back and know what I know now about football and recruiting, I had set a goal for myself that was highly unlikely. When I evaluate myself, I was NOT a Division I scholarship football player.

But my happiness and self-worth was linked to earning a scholarship.

In the end, I *did* earn a Division I football scholarship, but I believe there was a lot of luck behind this.

My point here is this—Set goals. Do everything you can to achieve them. Have the mindset that whatever the outcome may be, do not let that one thing dictate your happiness or self-worth.

The only thing you can control is that you put your best effort forward. If you do not achieve the goal you set, maybe it happened because you were being taught a lesson, maybe it happened because you were being taught how to fail. Embrace failure, for it is the only way we learn. Do not even call it failure. It is simply learning.

Failure as a challenge

Taking on challenges with the Growth Mindset is an essential element to improve. I have admitted before that playing football at Temple University was a reach for me. The challenge was great and I failed much more than I succeeded.

I remember one practice as a freshman there was a disgruntled upperclassmen put on the scout team. He lined up across from me, and for the next two hours, he threw me around the field like I was rag doll on roller skates. This was a severe beating that exposed many weaknesses about me as a player.

I will never forget this practice, since it was one of the most embarrassing moments of my life, especially because they film all the practices and you have to watch your misery again and again and again.

I recently saw this guy at an alumni game, and we talked about that exact practice. I had hated this guy up to the time we talked about it, but now I thank him for the challenge and helping me become better and learn from my mistakes. At the time, I had the Fixed Mindset. I resented this guy because I thought he was purposely trying to embarrass me. I let it get to me, and for weeks, I was distraught about this one practice.

If I had had the Growth Mindset at the time, I would have viewed this beating as a signal that I needed to do the following:

- Get stronger, so I had to get in the weight room and work my butt off.

- Learn my plays better so I could some off the ball without hesitation.
- Get tougher and not let one bad play dictate the next.

Challenges will come our way and there will be times where we are completely overwhelmed like I was at that practice. Every challenge in your life—success or failure—is opportunity.

- Opportunity to learn
- Opportunity to improve
- Opportunity to find out what exactly you need to do
-

Take on challenges in your life with the Growth Mindset and you will welcome them. Take them head on and allow them to shape who you are: a resilient, strong, and greatly improved individual.

My last football play

My last play in my 11-year football career ended when I found myself laying on the old school AstroTurf at Veterans Stadium with a broken leg.

My season was over and so was my football career. I was able to come back for another year of football but I decided not to play. What had been my entire life for the last 11 years would be over.

A lot went into my decision and it was the hardest one of my life, but something was calling me to move on from football.

I will be honest and tell that in my college years I was not the most focused student. My grades we very average and I hated my major. A message to all student athletes in college: You are there for an education first and to play sports second. This is something I cannot stress enough. Find something you love and follow it.

I knew that playing football at the next level would not be possible, and when I evaluated where I was at that point in my life, I knew I needed to make some changes. I was a business major that hated business, had no internships, had no experience and was not the least bit interested in going to work in a suit all day. I had spent four years in the classroom and had not much to show from it.

At the time I was 296 pounds and very uncomfortable in my skin. I wanted to lose weight and to lose it fast. During this time I fell in love with fitness. I read every magazine I could find and started to look into personal training certifications. Through my decision not to play football, I found a love for fitness and health.

Having the Growth Mindset is all about learning from mistakes, failures, and challenging times. It is taking the challenging times of your life and using them to help you become stronger and better and to find something you may not have been looking for.

It is about not letting mistakes and failure stop you from achieving what you want. I am not sure if I would have discovered this if my history had been different. If I did not have a football career filled with injures, maybe I would not be where I am today, doing something I love and being able to help people improve their lives.

Every event that seems challenging or heartbreaking at the time it occurs could be the start of something great, something even better than you ever imagined.

Turning failure into success

I am a good coach because I struggled as an athlete. In college, everything was hard. School was hard, football was hard, nothing came easy. I remember sitting in film sessions getting blasted by my coach for hours.

I remember one particular time in a film session after we played Maryland when I got absolutely crushed by one of the defensive tackles. I was literally lifted off my feet. The coach probably rewound that play 25 times.

"Vinny, you're out of position!"

"Vinny, did you even show up on this play?!"

"Vinny, you have really short arms!"

"Vinny, you just need to relax out there, you're trying too hard!"

It was embarrassing!

I am a good coach because I got coached so much. My deficits as a player turned into strengths as a coach. The athletes that went through their career and never struggled usually have a tough time being successful as a coach.

"Do it like I did it" is not a strategy that will usually work in coaching young athletes. Being a successful coach means bringing the best out of an athlete and helping him or her improve. It means understanding that people all process information differently and will learn in their own ways.

Every trainer on the GFP team was an athlete. None of us was a great athlete. All of us had lots of struggles in our athletic careers. These lessons made us better coaches. Our own struggles helped us identify what the majority of young athletes go through, and it has helped us be very effective in improving their performance and confidence.

There is only one thing we demand: Your best effort. Without your best effort your potential will not be reached. Everyone has the ability to improve at anything.

We take great pride in our profession as coaches, and we all use our experience to help our clients get better every day.

Your struggles shape you. Whatever struggles you have today are shaping you for your future. Embrace them, love them, learn from them.

Vince fails … again

"Failure is the tuition you pay for success."

On my way home from my Mastermind trip to Michigan, I purchased a copy of *Success Magazine*. This publication had come up several times during the weekend, and I wanted to grab a copy.

The theme of the entire publication was about failure. I found it funny how the magazine is titled *Success* and the main topic is failure. After reading several of the articles, I knew immediately that this was something I need to be reading consistently.

Each magazine comes with a CD. When I got home, I popped the CD in my car. On it were accounts of people who have had massive failure in their careers but have managed to recover and become successful.

The premise of the CD and many of the articles in the magazines was that we must treat failure as something that MUST occur for us to be successful. Many of them said things like they have learned to love failure, that failure is their friend. This attitude is exactly what the Growth Mindset talks about. Exactly.

I have failed more than you could ever imagine. I have failed so much I would need a few weeks to share all of my failures. After reading this magazine, I want to keep failing. I want to make mistakes. I want to fail. I want this because I know this is the only way I will get better.

You control how you view failure. You can let it define you and carry it with you, or you can embrace it as your friend and tell yourself that the day you fail is the day you get better, that it's one more step toward success.

There is no bigger failure rate than with dieting. People strive to lose weight, they lose a little, then they gain it back and then some. This seems to be a vicious cycle.

Every time this happens, there is a lesson. There is something you learned that will help you be more successful the next time, maybe a tip to lose more muscle than fat, maybe a way to actually keep the weight off. Either way, your failure is talking to you. It is giving you the answer of what *not to do*.

The key is to find these lessons and learn from them.

Keep failing.

If you never fail you never truly learn, and if you never learn, you never reach your true potential.

Get excited about failure. Embrace it.

More failure from *Success*

One morning recently, I was listening to the *Success Magazine* CD this morning on my way to Starbucks. It was raining, and for those of you who don't know me, I absolutely LOVE the rain. The rain makes me happy. For me, I get more and better work done in the rain, and the only time I actually like to run long distance is when it's raining out.

As I sat in my car and sipped my Starbucks bold, the CD started talking about failure. The magazine was interviewing the woman from *Shark Tank*, Barbara Corcoran, and she said the number-one success principle she looks for in an entrepreneur is the ability to get back up after a failure.

She did not say she was looking for someone who had never failed, just someone who can bounce back.

The amount of time it takes to respond to our failures is a key to success in any aspect of our lives. It is OK to get knocked down and sit there for a bit. There is nothing wrong with it. Some of us sit for five minutes, five hours, or five days.

As we go through our life, if we make the Growth Mindset part of our internal language, we will start to move toward the five-minute mark. Wouldn't it be nice and productive if, for any failure we had, we felt sorry for ourselves or dwelled upon the failure for only five minutes?

The Growth Mindset teaches us to learn from the times we get knocked down, to go through a process of why we failed and what we can do to improve. I have learned to love this process. Through practicing the Growth Mindset you will develop a love of learning and improvement.

It is OK to get knocked down. The key is how fast we get up and how hard we are working to get up even faster the next time. If you find yourself not being knocked down at all, you may be staying the same.

Growth is one of the highest-level human needs, along with contribution and love.

Get back up … and the next time get back up a little faster.

It's not that bad

We all inflate our own problems. Normally the things we consider problems will be gone in a day or are things that are in our power to fix. Are these real problems? No.

We inflate these problems because they are the biggest ones in front of us *right now*. The problem is that we get consumed by them.

I know there are many more people out there with bigger problems. Much bigger.

When we find ourselves getting paralyzed by issues we know will be over soon or things we have completely overreacted to, we need to think of the people that are going through real life-changing issues.

Think of them. And then ... go help them.

There is nothing that will help you stop feeling sorry for yourself quicker than helping someone else.

- Write them a really nice card
- Send a great text or email
- Go and visit them
- Cook them dinner
- Record a video message on your phone telling them you are thinking about them

So if you failed a test, are struggling to lose weight, lost a game, had a bad day at work, or just are ticked off about the weather ... get a grip!

Go and do something extraordinary for someone else. Make them feel amazing. I promise you that your own small issues will subside and you will get to make an impact on someone else.

Failure is the only way

I am not judged by the number of times I fail; I am judged by the number of times I succeed. The number of times I succeed is directly related to the number of times I fail and keep on trying.

Repeat this to yourself.

I am not judged by the number of times I fail; I am judged by the number of times I succeed. The number of times I succeed is directly related to the number of times I fail and keep on trying.

Once more ...

I am not judged by the number of times I fail; I am judged by the number of times I succeed. The number of times I succeed is directly related to the number of times I fail and keep on trying.

CHAPTER 4: LEARNING FROM MY FAMILY

I feel like everything I read these days talks about the Growth Mindset and the Fixed Mindset. The material does not always use these exact terms, but it is clearly talking about the Growth Mindset and the Fixed Mindset.

Growth Mindset: A way of thinking that enables someone to view all failure as a learning experience, to not take criticism personally, and to have an attitude that he or she can improve in anything.

Read that five times.

Fixed Mindset: A way of thinking that views failure as simply that: You failed, you are as you are, little improvement can be made so effort is not valued, and you take criticism personally.

As a parent now, I am constantly looking to improve my ability as a father. I never even thought about that before—teaching yourself to become a better parent—I always thought, "It just gets done."

It makes me think about everything else in life: work, sports, school, hobbies. It gives me so much joy to know that we are not stuck, that we can improve simply by striving to improve.

- I realize that having two daughters will be a challenge. (Or so everyone has told me!)
- I welcome and am excited for this challenge because I have the Growth Mindset.
- I have the view that every day is a day that has potential for me to become a better dad.
- I can improve my time management so it will give me more

time with the girls.

- I can read more books on parenting to help raise them with confidence and respect.
- I can talk to other more seasoned parents and ask their advice.
- I can keep learning about nutrition so I know the best foods for them to eat to be healthy, happy, and strong.
- I can work hard to improve my personal energy level so I can strongly accomplish all the things above.

I can only do all this if it is important to me. If you want to improve your health, it must be important to you. If you want to get better at sports, it must be important to you. Only then will you have the drive and focus to improve.

I am not afraid to fail because I have the Growth Mindset.

I am not afraid to not have the answer because I have the Growth Mindset.

If I fail, I am not failure. If I fail, I will not view myself as a bad father, just one that needs to improve.

Mimicry and completion

As a relatively new father, I am soaking in a lot of great information on how to master this parenting thing.

I realize that parents are leaders. Just as the head of a company is a leader, just as the coach of a team is a leader, and just as a teacher of a class is a leader, parents are leaders, too.

For a leader to be successful, he or she must *lead by example.*

As heads of the family, parents need to lead by example. This not only includes things like character or integrity, but also your language, mindset, tone of voice, and lastly, your health.

If you live an unhealthy life in regards to exercise and nutrition, there is a good chance your children will be the same way.

- If you eat sugar cereal or muffins at breakfast, there is a good chance your children will eat that too.
- If you work out very sporadically, there is a good chance your children will adopt the same routine.
- If you eat crappy snacks after dinner, there is a big chance your children will do that as an adult too.
- If you do not display the discipline to lose fat, there is a good chance your children will lack that same discipline.

There is a concept known as "mimicry and completion." (Warning: This might keep you up tonight when you think about this!)

Mimicry: You mimic your parents.

Completion: You complete your parents.

Here are a few of my personal examples.

Exercise

Growing up, I never really saw my dad exercise. When I was 22 years old, I almost lost my father to heart disease. This was exactly the time I was deciding whether to go into finance or become a personal trainer. That life experience catapulted me into making my career one of helping people to be healthy.

My father struggled with exercise his entire life. My decision to be in the health profession was my journey of completion.

Integrity

My father always told the truth. I always saw him as an honest businessman, and he would tell me how important it was to be a man of your word. He taught me through his actions and his words. To this day, I credit my mom and dad for their lessons on integrity.

Through mimicry, I have made integrity a strong point in my life.

Think about this process of mimicry and completion and now think about your children. What are the things do you want them to mimic that will help them be successful in their lives?

Lead by example and live a healthy life to set the tone for your children.

The Growth Mindset meets the terrible twos

I remember after my daughter Isabella turned two that we met a new baby in the house. Oh, her name was Isabella, but believe me, she was a completely different child!

Bella was starting to have tantrums. She started crying very easily when she did not get her way and would even drop to the floor to get more attention from us. I have been told this is completely normal, which made me feel better, but the first few days of this was crushing me and Vanessa.

Our thoughts were like:

How are we going to deal with this?

What did we do wrong?

Are we bad parents?

She is not even two years old yet!

I did what I do best and sought a solution through learning. We asked people with experience for advice, read a bunch of articles, and talked to our family.

We were and are still dealing with this but now with a different mindset. This type of situation is the perfect time to adopt a Growth Mindset. There is SO much learning going on in the life a toddler. It is learning at its finest.

As parents we can either have the mindset that we are raising a cranky kid who throws tantrums all the time or that we have a great challenge in front of us and we will put every effort forward to improve the situation.

We shifted our focus from shock and awe to learning and action. We learned, developed a strategy together, and are now implementing that strategy. There is less focus on the tantrums and more focus on our plan.

We have decided to let her have her tantrums. When she throws one, we ignore her until she stops. I know we have a long road in front of us, and we are probably just scraping the surface of issues like this, but I now felt so much more confident than I did a few weeks earlier.

We totally changed our mindset. Vanessa and I are learning. We are learning to be better parents and to deal with situations together and with a plan that is consistent.

Bella is also learning—she is learning that she is not the boss in the Gabriele home. From my experience thus far as a parent, I believe the Growth Mindset is more important than ever.

I can say this with extreme conviction that having the Growth Mindset as a parent may be the most important practice of all.

Toria's crib helps me remember something important

As my daughter Victoria got bigger, her crib needed to be lower. I've mentioned that I'm not much good at putting things together. Anything that requires instructions is a daunting task for me.

I remember from Bella's crib that lowering it was not much of a problem, so after the 18th time Vanessa asked me to do it, I was more than willing. The unfortunate part was that we did not have the proper wrench that was needed to lower it.

I am not going to point any fingers—Cough! Vanessa! Cough!—but let's just say it made it more difficult. The wrench I had was from Bella's crib, and it was too big, so I had to go into the garage and find some extra tools.

Thirty minutes into a 10-minute job I started to sweat. I even saw a drop of sweat fall from my forehead directly onto Victoria's mattress, poor little thing. I started to get frustrated and angry.

I then thought about what I was doing. I was lowering the crib of my healthy child.

I thought about my cousin who recently had a tragedy during the birth of one of his twins. I thought about him, and I thought about what he would do to be putting a crib together for that baby.

I thought about how much we all take for granted, that things like the health of our children are sometimes just expected.

It was a privilege to lower that crib yesterday.

Baby Bella and the Growth Mindset

Recently, I was working on the final touches of my presentations for our upcoming mentorship, during which we bring in trainers and business owners from around the country to learn about what we do at GFP.

Mindset was one of the main topics of my first presentation. Every time I work on this presentation, it brings me a deeper understanding of the Growth Mindset.

One of my main points will be to talk about Isabella, or any babies, for that matter.

Isabella has the Growth Mindset all the way. In fact, we are ALL born with the Growth Mindset, we are all born with mental toughness, we are all born with drive.

Somewhere along the road as young adults, these things change. We start worrying what others will think about us, we become afraid to make a mistake, we have thoughts of being inferior when we see others succeed.

Please do not think that because I write about the Growth Mindset that I always have it. In fact, over that weekend while I was writing, several times I found myself having the Fixed Mindset. The key is that we do our best to practice the Growth Mindset.

We must have an awareness about it and be able to quickly self-regulate.

Isabella does not worry that Vanessa and I might be upset with her for not walking yet.

She will walk when she is ready to walk and has no feeling of being inferior. She is just living her life: laughing, smiling, crying, falling, sleeping, and eating.

She does not have an inner voice that says things like, "That kid over there is 10 months old and is walking already. I am almost 14 months and have not walked yet. What is wrong with me?"

It just doesn't happen.

Our goal with Isabella is to not mess this up. Yes, there will be challenges, but we know it is possible for ALL of us to have the Growth Mindset simply because we are born with it!

✓ Do

Treat mistakes as opportunities to learn

👎 Do Not

Feel inferior when you see others succeeding

✓ Do

Practice the Growth Mindset

👎 Do Not

Think you will have it all the time

✓ Do

Recognize quickly the Fixed Mindset and adapt

👎 Do not

Worry what others think

✓ Do

Believe you can improve at anything!

Baby Bella walks!

Yes, baby Bella had a little trouble getting started with walking. Well, after many failures, falls, and mistakes, Bella is motoring around the house. She still falls all the time but she gets better every day.

She walks with a wide base to help keep her balance and kind of looks like Vanessa when she walks at eight-plus months pregnant.

The Growth Mindset teaches us to learn from our failures, to gather information when we do fail, document it in our brain, and then use that information on future attempts to become more successful.

This phenomenon was going on inside the little brain of Isabella, and I am sorry to say she did not learn it from me or Vanessa.

She was born with it. She was born with drive, mental toughness, perseverance, and the Growth Mindset. We are all born with it. Somewhere along the way we lose it. Even if we have lost our drive, perseverance, and mental toughness, the Growth Mindset tells us we can get it back.

It will not be easy, but we can get these things back. The first step is realizing that everyone in this world has failed. NO one is perfect.

Michael Jordan, Albert Einstein, Thomas Edison, Benjamin Franklin, W. A. Mozart—all have failed much more than we could ever imagine.

Failure is good. It is how we learn and how we improve. I now embrace failure with one thing: opportunity, the opportunity to learn.

I still get very upset when I fail, but it only lasts a very short time. Then my Growth Mindset kicks on and I am good.

Embrace failure. It is your best chance to get better!

"Hard work beats talent when talent fails to work hard."

— Kevin Durant

Boring reader

I was reading to Bella recently. We were reading the story of Moses and I guess it was boring her. Instead of listening, she kept asking questions about the pictures. "Who's that? What's that?"

I was getting frustrated thinking, why the heck is this kid not listening to the story? I then realized that I was the problem. (Imagine that!)

I realized I was tired from a long day and reading in a monotone voice, not bringing any real enthusiasm to the book. *I* was boring, not the book. So instead of listening to boring me, she started asking questions about the story. I don't blame her.

It made me think of two things:

1. If situations are not going the way we planned, take a look in the mirror first.

You may be the problem.

- That job that isn't working out
- The teacher that keeps coming down on you
- The coach that has it out for you
- The spouse that just won't give you a break
-

Before making any decisions, do some self-reflection and ask yourself if your actions may be contributing to the problem.

2. Bring energy into whatever you do

I never changed what I was doing. I was reading the story of Moses the entire time. The story didn't all of a sudden get better, *I* did. I started reading the book with enthusiasm, and believe it or not, she stopped asking questions and started listening to the great story. She was engaged by how I was reading the story because I changed my tone, outlook, and energy.

Where do you need to show up in your life with more energy and enthusiasm?

Two lessons from Vanessa Gabriele

Last Easter Sunday was exactly one year that my best friend, Karen, was taken from us way too soon. She was a beautiful, smart, caring, 32-year-old woman about to begin her next journey when a rare form of cancer took her within six months.

Four days after she passed, Vincent and I were blessed with our second daughter, Victoria Karen. That week was a whirlwind of emotions.

This experience has driven me to be an all-around better wife, mom, friend, and daughter. I promised myself that I would live a better life for her and continue to honor her in any way I can. Our life is a beautiful journey, and it will take unexpected twists and turns, but every day, I try to remind myself, are you just living? Or are you alive?!

We all have our days where we are dragging, exhausted or just get in that Fixed Mindset that it can be hard to get yourself out of.

Missing my girlfriend KK every day, I have realized the importance of these two goals:

1. *Be grateful*

A friend of ours shared something with us that really has helped me. Set your alarm for every four hours or so and title it "*What's perfect?*"

In that exact moment, you realize the simplest things to be grateful for: "I'm healthy, my kids are outside playing, and I took time to work out."

It just makes you step out of that moment and makes you look at the positive things in your life that you are grateful for.

2. *Be Compassion It*

We all strive to be great examples for our children.

I have found a way honor Karen's life and hopefully make this world a better place for our children. I came across a nonprofit organization called Compassion It. As a part of Compassion It, you wear a bracelet every day.

The bracelet is black on one side and white on the other. You start the day with the bracelet on the dark side. When you have done something that exhibits compassion, you flip it to the white side.

Random acts of kindness go a long way, and paying it forward can only make us better. Gabriele Fitness strives to create a healthy lifestyle for families, both mentally and physically.

This bracelet serves as a reminder of how far a simple random act of kindness can go. Whether it's just a smile, a hug, letting someone go in front of you, or reaching out to someone with a thank you note or a phone call, do something for someone else every day.

CHAPTER 5: LESSONS FOR YOUR BRAIN

You know I'm a health and fitness coach, so my nominal focus is on the body. But in my reading, everything seems to come back to the brain. After all, what is the brain but the most important part of the body?

In order for us to be the most productive we can be as professionals, parents, and students, it is essential to have a basic knowledge of our brain. I am going to do my best to teach you about the brain in the most basic terms possible.

The brain is an incredible organ and we are the only living species on earth to have certain functions in our brains.

Back in the cave man days, our brains were just like animals brains.

It went like this:

- Me see, me eat.
- Me see, me kill.

There was no process of rationalization.

As we have evolved as a species, we have actually created a new part of the brain, probably the most important part. It sits behind your forehead and makes up only four to five percent of our brain, but it packs a very powerful punch.

It is called the pre-frontal cortex. This is the part of the brain that helps us make decisions and solve problems. It is responsible for things like setting goals, controlling impulses, visualization, and creative thinking, and it is where we hold our thoughts.

I would like you to think about your pre-frontal cortex like a stage in a play. This stage is limited in size and needs a lot of lighting (energy) to function. The actors in the play represent the outside information coming in to your brain in the form of emails, conversations, and other input.

Power to light this stage is a limited resource. Oxygen and glucose are what fuel the pre-frontal cortex. The pre-frontal cortex chews up this fuel very quickly, meaning that your capacity to think is a very limited resource.

This is why prioritizing is so important. When you prioritize, it is very taxing to your brain. This is why it needs to be done while your stage is clear. If there are too many actors on the stage, we lack the ability to prioritize and think clearly.

Here is a suggestion: prioritize prioritizing.

This means to think about your priorities or what is most important to accomplish early in the day. If you are going to write a to-do list, do it first thing in the AM while your stage is clear.

Mindset is all about our thoughts. If we understand how our brain works, we can better manage and control them.

Willpower: Got any?

Willpower might very well be the key to success in almost every aspect of improvement. We do not fail in our quest to lose fat due to a lack of information. Everyone knows that a salad with chicken is better for losing fat than a bowl of spaghetti and meatballs. But why do we lack the willpower to make these decisions consistently?

As a friend of mine has written, the only thing that must be present for a diet to work is consistency. I will talk further about willpower throughout this book, but first let's define what willpower actually is:

- Willpower is the ability to delay gratification, resisting short-term temptations in order to meet long term goals.
- The capacity to override an unwanted thought or feeling or impulse.

If we really want to know more about willpower we must look at some basic brain function.

There are two main areas of the brain that influence our willpower:

- The limbic system
- The pre-frontal cortex

The limbic system is our emotional brain. It controls things like motivation, drive and urges. The pre-frontal cortex is the logical part of our brain. This is our cognitive function, rational thought, and reasoning.

Whenever an emotional response (What's to eat?) is generated by our limbic system, the pre-frontal cortex interprets that response. If our pre-frontal cortex is strong and active, it will help us make reasonable decisions (salad with chicken over spaghetti and meatballs).

In order to have a lot of willpower, we need a strong pre-frontal cortex.

It is just like with our bodies—if we lift weights consistently, our muscles will get stronger. If we don't, they will be weak. Making the tough decisions to choose the healthy food over the bad food is what helps our pre-frontal cortex get stronger.

Think about the times where you were on a roll with your nutrition. After a few days, you probably did not crave crappy food nearly as much. This situation means your pre-frontal cortex is getting stronger.

If we choose to eat bad food consistently, it does not train our willpower muscles, leaving our pre-frontal cortex weak and small. This makes bad decisions easy.

In other words, doing the things we simply feel like doing does not give our pre-frontal cortex the training it needs to give us the willpower that will help us be successful. Having more willpower will justify the decision to choose the salad over the spaghetti.

So ...

Other than simply making the right decisions, how do we help our pre-frontal cortex get stronger?

Optimal sleep

One of the most important things you can do to improve the function of your pre-frontal cortex and get more willpower is to get proper sleep. If you want to have less willpower and a poorly functioning pre-frontal cortex, then get six hours or less of sleep.

The pre-frontal cortex gets crushed without adequate sleep and loses control over the region of your brain that create cravings and the stress response. This means that your brain overreacts to normal stressful situations and temptations.

According to Dr. James Mass of Cornell University, adults need between seven-and-a-half and eight-and-a-half hours of sleep per night. Getting less than this drastically reduces willpower.

Studies show that not getting adequate sleep has a similar effect on your brain as being slightly drunk. Imagine going through life slightly drunk all the time... Some of us are.

Too much caffeine and sleep

One of my past addictions was with caffeine. Caffeine gives you willpower. Good, right? No. What happens is when you rely on too much caffeine for your natural willpower, the function of the pre-frontal cortex is compromised

Based on my research this rule will help tremendously:

NO CAFFEINE AFTER 2 p.m.

There is a half-life for caffeine of about six hours. For example, a cup of coffee with about 200 milligrams of caffeine consumed at 3 p.m. will have half of its caffeine, or about 100 milligrams, still be in your system at 9 p.m.

What does this mean?

Even if you can fall asleep at 9 p.m., the caffeine is still in your system and your sleep quality will be compromised.

But why?

This is because you will never get to the most important stage in your sleep cycle, called the rapid eye movement stage, or REM sleep.

What are the benefits of REM sleep?

- Boosts mood during the day
- Essential for processing and consolidating emotions (WILLPOWER!)
- Vital to learning and developing new skills

My willpower, brain function, sleep quality, energy, and health have improved dramatically after I become non-dependent on caffeine.

Tapping the prioritized brain through WILLPOWER!

The more and more I read about success, the more I learn about the human brain. It is an absolutely extraordinary thing. The human brain consumes one-fifth of the calories we burn for energy but is only about one-fiftieth of our body mass. Incredible!

Most of our conscious activity happens in our pre-frontal cortex. The pre-frontal cortex is responsible for focus, handling short-term memory, solving problems and moderating impulse control. It is the most responsible part of the brain, and it provides us with willpower.

Here is what you need to know about willpower.

Think of it like the battery on your cell phone. In the morning, you have full power. As the day goes on and you use your phone, the power goes down.

Willpower works exactly the same way. Willpower is depleted throughout your day as you make decisions, suppress feelings and impulses, or change your behavior to achieve your goals.

The first step in having willpower is understanding that it is an exhaustible resource.

If we lose willpower, use the Growth Mindset and understand that willpower is something that can and will be refueled.

One of the reasons why I always read and write first thing in the morning is because my willpower tank is full and I get great work done during this time. Reading and writing are very important tasks in my life, and they deserve a full tank of my willpower.

Four willpower tips

- Use your willpower on the things that matter most to you and do those things early in the day.
- Realize that willpower is an exhaustible resource and that you only have so much of it.
- Try to focus on one thing at a time and do that one thing very well.
- Recharging your willpower with downtime and relaxation is imperative to continue towards your goals.

Why Vince quit drinking coffee

Since 2003, I have taken some form of caffeine. Whether it was coffee, energy drinks, or supplements, I have taken it all. I am not proud of it, and I realized one day how addicted I was.

I was getting on a flight to go to a conference and did not have my morning coffee. Later that day I started to feel almost sick, had no motivation, and had a headache that had me seeing stars.

This was when I knew how much I depended on it. I have accomplished a lot in the last 12 years, but all at the expense of becoming dependent on caffeine.

I recently quit drinking caffeine for 11 days. It was VERY hard and left me irritable and much less motivated to work hard. I was so interested in how addicted I was that I started researching it. I found out that addiction to caffeine is a pretty serious issue.

The goal here is not to get you to never to drink coffee but to help you understand that being dependent on it is problematic. It can lead to other health issues such as anxiety, adrenal fatigue, and cardiovascular issues, among others.

In my research, I found that consuming 500 to 600 milligrams of caffeine is very excessive. My advice is to not go out and have 499.9 milligrams a day and think you are in the clear! (Don't worry, it crossed my mind too.)

It stated that 300 milligrams (three normal size cups of coffee) or less is a safe amount. Everyone is different and will respond differently.

Remember! Even if you only have one cup a day, if you have severe symptoms when you go a few days without, that means you need to cut back.

After a talk with my acupuncturist Roberto Andrade about this issue, he basically told me that caffeine improves willpower. When you are dependent on the caffeine to work harder or get more done, your natural willpower weakens. This is why when you get off caffeine, you don't want to do that much. Your willpower is taken from you.

I needed my natural willpower back.

I took 11 days off caffeine and now am back having one small homebrewed quality cup of coffee a day. I feel so much better.

My goal is to never go over two cups, not have a regular Starbucks habit, and NOT be dependent on it. Meaning, if I run out of coffee I do not want to smash anyone.

I used to get a venti Starbucks every morning and would many times get an afternoon fix as well—no more for me. I estimate that I will save close to $1,000 this year from not going to Starbucks regularly.

Bottom line: Please learn from my mistakes and get back to using your natural willpower. I promise you will think more clearly, sleep better, and be much healthier.

How elephants can help you reach your goals

When I was playing football at Temple I weighed close to 300 pounds. In order to maintain this weight I had to eat everything in sight in very large quantities.

I had to be 300 pounds, because there was a guy on the other side of the ball that was just as big who was trying to kill our quarterback—the guy I was trying to protect.

Being huge was a necessity to be able to compete as an offensive lineman.

After football I needed to make changes.

There was no longer a reason for me to be 300 pounds, and although I always exercised, my eating choices needed to change. This was not an easy task. (I got very used to eating four plates of food at every meal.)

I am sure many of you need to make changes too. Maybe you eat and drink too much on the weekend and it hinders your overall progress. Maybe you only workout one to two times per week and know you need three to four workouts. Maybe you stress about everything and it affects your relationship with your family.

We all have things in our life we need to change.

After re-reading a game-changing book called *Switch: How to Change Things When Change Is Hard* by Chip and Dan Heath, I want to share a great analogy called the Elephant and the Rider. When examining behavioral change, think of an elephant and someone riding the elephant trying to follow a certain path.

The Elephant

The elephant is a powerful, stubborn creature that represents our emotional side, the side looking for a quick payoff rather than long-term benefits (the voice that tells you to skip the workout today because there is always tomorrow).

The Rider

The rider represents our rational side that knows what should be done and can tug on the reigns of the elephant to instill a small degree of control over it (the voice that says I am working out today, no matter what).

The Path

The path represents the situation in which the change is to take place (the decision to exercise three to four times per week instead of two).

Implementing change is like riding an elephant: Choose a direction (goal), give your elephant some peanuts (motivation), and stick to an easy path.

Now that you have a clearer picture of change, here is one strategy to take with you today:

Most people fail because they give themselves too big of a mountain to climb (too big of a change). Picture an elephant staring up at a huge mountain he needs to climb. The result will be that the elephant will do anything possible NOT to have to climb that huge mountain.

But what if it was just a small hill? He could do that!

In order to make changes, focus on small wins. If your goal is to change your habit of eight workouts a month to 12, start with nine workouts a month, then progress to 10.

Big changes require small easy wins.

Breathing

Having a second child is no joke. I remember a point when our daughters were 17 months and six weeks old. Things were wonderfully hectic around here. Everything just seemed a little busier, a little more challenging, and a little more stressful. We are so happy with our new family, but it is not easy.

I have been finding myself getting stressed out more frequently. My mindset has been challenged in the last few months, and I sometimes I forget that challenging times are simply learning experiences for the future.

The struggles we go through now are what help us in the future. If you go through your entire athletic career with no injuries, no setbacks, no losses, no bad coaches, and no adversity, then you are probably not playing. These things will happen, and it is what we learn from them that will help us to be more successful.

From this time, I have learned that when I get stressed out that diaphragm breathing helps me tremendously.

Breathing has helped my mindset.

It calms you down, gives you a minute to think and process what is going on, and places you into a more parasympathetic state, that is, it promotes calmness. Dedicating five minutes a day to practicing your breathing will make a huge difference make in your quality of life and your mindset.

Using this technique will do wonders for your health too. Here is a list of the benefits, as recommended by the Mayo Clinic:

- Relieves physical muscle tension

- Allows the mental function to slow and relax

- Body and mind connection

- Calms and centers

- Activates parasympathetic nervous system

- Releases natural wastes, such as carbon dioxide

- Gives the internal organs a gentle massage

- Increases the oxygen to all cells

- Strengthens the lungs

- Slows your heart rate

- Lowers your blood pressure

- Increases blood flow to muscles

- Improves concentration

- Reduces anger and frustration

- Boosts confidence

There's a great video from my friend Michelle about learning to breathe at www.youtube.com/watch?v=LnWSr3_m5EY.

Vince's life-changing experience

I recently added a new component to my morning routine. For close to two months I have been meditating daily, sometimes twice a day.

As someone with a lot on my plate such as running a business and having a pretty busy family life, my brain always seemed to be going. Stress was clouding my head and impairing my ability to think clearly. This negatively impacted my performance as a leader, father, husband, and coach.

When I added daily meditation to my routine, this all changed. I am able to focus more. I now can take a step back and think about the big picture, and it is much clearer!

- I have less stress
- I am more patient
- My body feels better physically
- My workouts are better
- I am a better husband and father
- I listen more
- I can read longer and retain more information
- I am happier

If you have not read the book *The Power of Habit: Why We Do What We Do in Life and Business*, by Charles Duhigg, I strongly recommended you read it. The book talks about keystone habits.

A keystone habit is more important than other habits because they create positive changes that spill into other areas. Exercise is a keystone habit.

Here is a typical pattern:

- *Start an Exercise program at GFP ☺ (the keystone habit)*
- Start eating better
- Start sleeping better
- Start having more energy
- Start being more in the moment with family
- Start doing more things for others
- Start having a happier more fulfilled life

I firmly believe meditation is a keystone habit that, if adopted, will bring on many more positive things into your life.

My new secret brain weapon

In addition to the keystone habit of meditation, I've discovered another brain weapon that has my brain functioning at an all-time high.

About every other week, I have been going into a sensory deprivation tank for about 90 minutes at a time. It is a large pod filled with 10 inches of salt water. The salt water makes you float, making your body totally weightless. Being weightless helps decreases physical pain because it completely de-loads your body.

Even when you are sitting on a comfortable couch, you are still using muscles, tendons, and ligaments to maintain your posture. In the tank, all of this tension is completely off your body. So physically I feel better.

But the biggest improvement I have seen is with my stress level, mental clarity, and focus. I have gotten Vanessa hooked on floating too. She said with two kids, patience can get low, and after two sessions of floating, she noted a dramatic improvement.

Although there is minimal research on floating, I am believer and am hooked. If you can find somewhere near you that offers floating, I recommend it!

CHAPTER 6: TAPPING THE MIND

Is the mind different from the brain? I'm going to leave that one for the philosophers, but for me, the brain is about chemistry and physiology, while the mind is what we do with all that brain matter. Here we get into *psychology*, like sports psychology, the psychology of being a parent, business psychology, and so on. These are a few of my thoughts.

Setting goals is the first step in turning the invisible into visible.
— Tony Robbins

Setting goals

What gives Olympic athletes the ability to work so hard for so long? They train for four years and most do not miss a day of training, a meal, a practice, or even a mental preparation session. They simply do everything they need to do for four years straight.

Yes, many are gifted athletes who have been playing their sport their entire lives, but there is something more powerful that is going on.

They have a clearly defined goal. All the work they are doing is going into ONE event, the Olympic Games. They will do everything in their power to prepare themselves the best they can for this one event. They know exactly what they want.

In life, one of the most beneficial things we can do is to have written goals. In fact, only about three percent of adults have their goals written down on paper.

It is important that your goals are written down. Writing is a psychoneuromotor activity that forces you to think and concentrate. That is why taking notes when you read is so important—it helps you retain the information. Writing puts things in your conscious mind, so you will always be thinking about it.

Your brain has a success or a failure mechanism. The success mechanism is triggered by a goal. The failure mechanism is the temptation to follow the undisciplined path of least resistance. The failure mechanism is also triggered by procrastination.

Procrastination is the thief in life!

We are purpose-driven beings. Happiness comes when we are in control, when you have a clear goal that you are working toward each day.

Here are four easy steps to set your goals:

- Decide what you want
- Write it down
- Set a deadline
- Do something every day that moves you one step closer to your goal

The statistics are evident that very few people actually achieve the goals they set. The biggest reason is too many big changes that require too much willpower.

Here is a typical New Year's resolution list:

- I want to get into the best shape of my life this year

- I will go to the gym every day
- I will eat perfectly and never cheat
- I will get nine hours of sleep every night
- I will give to charity more

This is a guaranteed failure for many reasons.

Here is an example of one that worked:

Last year I had a goal of drinking one cup of coffee per day. The reason was to take in less caffeine. The purpose was to improve my health so I could have more consistent energy to be with my family.

Linking a goal to a bigger purpose is a key ingredient for success.

My strategy was using a 16-ounce mug that I filled to the very top! I achieved that goal over the year. My strategy for the following year is the same with one small adjustment.

I will use a 12-ounce cup this year. It's only four ounces less—easy, right? You can do that!

But let's do some math. I drink coffee 365 days per year. This comes to 1,460 fewer ounces of coffee in 2015. This equates to 36,500 milligrams LESS caffeine. All I did was change the cup.

When selecting goals, the key word is consistency. My challenge is for you to make only very small changes, stay consistent, and see the results.

Usual response: But I am consistent for a month and then I fall off the wagon!

The key to staying on the wagon is making it easy. I am not stopping drinking coffee. That would be a disaster. Headaches, low energy— no way.

But I can change my cup, no problem.

Make it easy. Easy wins. Easy is what brings consistency.

Your ONE thing

I have a friend named Dr. Rob Gilbert. He is a sports psychologist at Montclair State University. I have so much respect for Dr. Gilbert for the tremendous success he has achieved in his life and for the number of people he has made an impact on.

Dr. Gilbert has a success hotline. He records a 3-minute motivational message (on a cassette tape recorder) … every day, Monday through Sunday. It's not two minutes or four minutes. It's three minutes … every time.

It's not Monday through Saturday and take off Sunday. It's Monday through Sunday … every week.

But the most impressive thing to me is that he has recorded over 8,000 messages over a 23-plus-year span … and has never missed a day. This is the ultimate example of consistency.

It's no secret that being consistent is a key to success in living a healthy life.

This is why we hate diets at GFP. It's very hard to be on a diet the rest of your life. You don't have to be perfect 100 percent of the time. This is not realistic. You just need to be good most of the time. It's much easier to stay in shape than to get in shape.

Here is the key to being more consistent:

Make it easy.

If it's easy, you'll do it.

If you do it consistently for 66 days, it becomes a habit, and then it becomes automatic. When it becomes automatic, you use much less willpower, and that gives you the ability to do more good things with less effort.

What's ONE really easy thing you can do for 66 days in a row that will improve your health?

Here are some examples, but please pick your own:

- Maybe it's drink half your body weight in ounces of water
- Maybe it's add one more workout a week
- Maybe it's get 30 more minutes of sleep per night
- Maybe it's meditate for 10 minutes a day
- Maybe it's have one greens drink a day
- Maybe it's starting to drink a protein shake after your workouts
- Maybe it's recording your food daily

Pick ONE THING that YOU know is EASY for you that will improve your health, and be sure to notice that each thing listed above is *measurable*.

Pick ONE THING and start it tomorrow … No, wait, start it today.

Getting better

Focus on getting better rather than being good. Many times, we will focus on being good at something more than focusing on getting better.

If we are in a constant state of striving to improve, we will ultimately be much more successful in the long run.

When I was in third grade, I was a great baseball player. I would crush homeruns, strike out everybody, and make great plays at short stop. This initial success was my biggest downfall in my baseball career.

Every year I got worse. The reason was that my focus was just on how many homeruns I could hit, not improving my skills as a baseball player. I was good, and my focus was to keep being good, not on continual improvement.

A laser focus on only being good puts you in a position to compare yourself with others versus comparing yourself with your own performance. I was better than most and I accepted it. If I was looking to truly get better, I should have looked to improve my own performance each year by practicing hitting, throwing, and fielding.

After a while, just showing up at the games did not bring me much success. In fact, many of the other players started to outplay me.

Each year, I played I became less well until I eventually stopped playing baseball.

Whatever it is you do, have your focus be on getting better rather than making sure others think you are good.

Talking to your children about getting better

I have always loved the concept of the Growth Mindset. It always seemed right. After doing some much deeper research into the Growth Mindset, I have discovered that it is entrenched in proven science.

If you're interested in the Growth Mindset, you should be thinking about how to speak to your children using Growth Mindset language

Here is a VERY short summary of a study I read about:

Research Study 1

A group of fifth graders were given a series of puzzles. The puzzles were very easy to finish, the reason being so all the kids would do well.

When the researchers told the kids their score, they praised one group for being smart ("You must be smart at this.") and the other group for their effort ("You must have really worked hard on this.").

Research Study 2

Then the kids were given a choice for their second test:

- A hard problem, where they were told they would learn a lot from attempting it

OR

- An easy one, just like the first

Ninety percent of the kids praised for EFFORT chose the hard one.

The majority of the kids praised for being SMART choose the easy one.

Research Study 3

Then, all the students were given a very hard test, the purpose of which was to induce failure among all students. The students praised for their EFFORT welcomed the challenge, getting very involved in the process and attempting to try many solutions to the puzzles.

The students praised for being SMART were sweating and miserable.

Research Study 4

After inducing a round of failure, they gave all of the students another easy test, similar to the one in Study 1.

The kids praised for being SMART did 20 percent worse than they did originally.

The kids praised for their EFFORT did 30 percent better.

Here is the big takeaway

When we praise for EFFORT, we reward the process, not the result. When we praise for effort, we give kids a variable that they are in control of regarding their success.

Praising for being SMART or talented takes this control away.

Praising for effort helps kids take on more challenges. Instead of getting anxious when things get hard, they get excited about the potential things they will learn.

As parents and coaches, we can help. Next time a kid wins a game or aces a test, reward them for the effort and hard work they put into that accomplishment

Tell them, "Wow, you must be really proud of all the hard work you put into that."

It's a game changer.

Adventures in the wagon

Recently I took my two girls on a long adventure. I loaded them up in a wagon and we walked around the entire town of New Providence. It took us about two hours.

We stopped at my grandma's house to say hello, but I quickly realized it was a bad idea. The kids almost broke everything in the house. (It's amazing how many little breakable things she had lying around!)

On the walk home, we hit a street that sent me back about 30 years. From first through sixth grade I used to walk home, every day. I remember every crack in the sidewalk on this street, I knew it so well.

For some reason, as I was dragging my kids up this hill, I started getting emotional. I was always the big kid in class. I had a different desk than all the other kids and always remember being labeled the big kid—many times this meant the fat kid.

I remember this hill very well. I remember walking up it crying after I got teased at school. I remember going up it after getting sent to the principal's office. I remember walking up it after failing another test.

But most of all I remember this—Many times I would ride my bike. I was not able to ride my bike the entire way up the hill. I always had to get off and walk it because it was just too hard. I always felt embarrassed when people I knew would honk at me as they drove by and I was walking my bike up the hill.

As I was dragging my two children up in the wagon with no real struggle, I thought back to those days. How could a fat kid that couldn't ride his bike up a hill be a fitness professional that has helped thousands of people get healthy?

It seemed impossible at the time, like many things in our lives.

Where we are right now is simply a series of choices we have made. Where we are right now is not a picture of where we can be. It's just the start.

Maybe you are a bad student right now. Maybe you hate school. I know I did. But that does mean you cannot be successful in your life or become a *better* student. Maybe you have no discipline with your nutrition, maybe you eat well for a few days, and then one meal sends you flying off the horse.

This only tells the story of today. Do not let where you are right now influence the possibilities of the future. Maybe you can't lose weight no matter what you try.

A fat kid that couldn't ride his bike up the hill has a different message:

You can't lose weight ... yet. When you can't do something, use this.

You can't do it ... YET.

Effort

Many times, we view asking for help as a personal defect. We see it as not being capable of something ourselves, so we must seek help to achieve something we want.

I remember when I was younger that I was constantly in and out of reading and math tutors for extra help. I often had the feeling that I did this so much that I was not smart enough to be able to succeed without them. This is Fixed Mindset thinking.

Seeking extra help, whether it is business advice or tutoring, is an effort to improve and should be viewed this way. Effort needs to be looked at as something that is positive and necessary to succeed, not that you have a defect if you have to try very hard to succeed.

If you have to stay after school for extra help or after practice for additional technique work, you should not view your effort here as having trouble but rather that you are making a solid effort to improve in school and your sport.

The Fixed Mindset views effort as fruitless because there is not an assured success.

I will tell you that even after all the tutors, I was still an average student. I am not sure where I would be now math-wise without those tutors, but I did learn that it is OK to need help. I learned that many times, things will not come easy, and there are extra things we may need to do in order to just break even.

It is never a negative to have to try very hard. There are more important lessons behind your tutoring sessions that you do not realize at the time, but the sequence of having trouble, working extra hard, improving, and then using the entire process as a learning experience is well worth the extra effort you put in.

The one question you MUST ask yourself

Last week Vanessa and I took a much-needed vacation without the kids. During our time away, I read three books:

- *No Easy Day: The Firsthand Account of the Mission that Killed Osama bin Laden*, by Mark Owen
- *Positive Time-Out: And Over 50 Ways to Avoid Power Struggles in the Home and the Classroom*, by Jane Nelsen
- *Turning Pro: Tap Your Inner Power and Create Your Life's Work*, by Steven Pressfield

One pleasure read, one parenting read, and one personal development. I started a fourth book on the plane called *The Checklist Manifesto*, by Atul Gawande.

There is something going on with my brain. I am reading faster. I comprehend better. I am able to read much longer without being distracted.

My brain has been training. Lumosity is working. Two of the books I read indirectly talked about the Growth Mindset.

Jane Nelsen mentioned probably 20 times in her book *Positive Time-Out* about how little children need to make mistakes. It's the best way for them to learn.

Pressfield talked about how true professionals all fail throughout their entire career. He mentions the time when he turned pro that he was not doing great work but to actually just sit down and do his work. In his failure, he learned he just needed to get started!

It seems that no matter where I go, people talk about how important it is to learn from mistakes or failure, yet so many still find it so hard.

Let me make this simple for you with one question.

Whenever something happens—you're cut from a team, fail a test, miss a workout, drop the ball on something important, lose a job, can't find a job, get injured, do not meet a goal—ask yourself this one question every time.

What have I learned from this experience that can make me better tomorrow?

Have this question memorized and ask it to yourself often. There is always something to learn, especially in the toughest of times. Bring this question into your life and focus on improvement instead of how we feel about our failures.

Optimism

"You are 100 percent responsible for how you choose to respond to everything that happens in your life."

— Unknown

One week, Victoria had a fever, so I stayed home with her while Vanessa took Bella out. As soon as she left, Victoria fell asleep on my chest.

I started and finished what was one the greatest short books I have ever read. It was an audio book that lasted about 90 minutes.

The book was called *Learned Optimism: How to Change Your Mind and Your Life*, by Martin E. P. Seligman. I learned something really important from the book that I'd like to share. I think you'll find it useful:

When we are optimistic, it is similar to having a Growth Mindset. When we are pessimistic, it's similar to the Fixed Mindset.

Crushing pessimism is imperative to living a longer and happier life. It is proven in research that optimists are healthier and live longer than pessimists.

So here is a strategy to crush Pessimism.

Distraction

When we have negative thoughts that take place in our pre-frontal cortex, it has the tendency to take over our minds. Creative, productive, and high-performance work is compromised when this takes place.

When you think a negative thought, distract yourself with something. The book suggests slapping a wall and yelling STOP, or having a rubber band on your wrist and snapping it.

Distraction is great during sporting events because it can help get your mind off a bad play you just had. The distraction gets you out of that pessimistic thought process and will help prepare you for the next play.

I like the rubber band idea. Let's say you fell off your healthy eating plan and had a piece of cake. I can hear you now saying, "I just have no discipline," or "I never can stick to a diet." Snap that rubber band on your wrist and tell yourself that you are one meal away from being back on track.

CHAPTER 7: SEALFIT

Last year I participated in something called SEALFIT. SEALFIT is a one-day version of Navy SEAL Hell Week. Navy SEAL Hell Week is normally five days straight of no sleeping, the most grueling physical training one can endure. It's basically about trying to find a mindset that you can do 20 times what you think you are capable of.

Seventy to eighty percent of the people that enter Navy SEAL Hell Week do not complete it. You do not have to be a Navy SEAL to do SEALFIT, but you must be willing to train like one for a day. The instructors that ran our day were real Navy SEALs at one point in their career, and they treated us exactly like we were in Hell Week.

Before I tell you my SEALFIT story, let me give you a little background. I am part a small group of guys in the fitness industry. We decided to do this all together to help build a stronger bond between us and do something that would take our mindset to a level we have never been.

SEALFIT was our Answer.

We trained for this for almost four months. It consumed our bodies and our minds. The sacrifices we all made were immense, but in the end we are forever stronger.

Preparing for SEALFIT

When I decided to accept the invitation to do SEALFIT, I really had no idea what I was getting into. I am *NOT* a runner and I hadn't run more than 200 yards in a long time, with the exception of a few charity 5Ks that took me an ungodly amount of time.

SEALFIT requires you to be able to run and run for a long time, carrying a pack filled with 10 percent of your bodyweight. I remember being nervous about running for the first time because I knew that my conditioning was so poor.

The first time I tested it was while walking the dog in the morning. I started to jog and immediately started to breathe heavy. I probably went for three minutes and stopped. I knew I was not in great running shape, but I did not think I was this bad.

I had so much work to do and only about three-and-a-half months to do it. That first week I had this overwhelming feeling like, what did I get myself into? Negative thoughts consumed my day.

I needed help. I hired a coach from Seattle who is an expert in training MMA athletes. He also happens to be the inventor of a heart rate variability product that measures the fatigue of your nervous system, a very important factor when training hard.

He wrote my program and got me started. I followed it to a "t." This gave me great peace of mind. I was not nervous anymore; I was just going to do everything coach told me to do to the best of my ability, and whatever happened would happen.

Now I just focused on working hard instead of worrying if I would be prepared enough.

At SEALFIT, I did well. I made it through the entire 12-plus-hour day and could have kept going. The running was never a problem and I actually found myself at the front of the pack many times.

Sometimes a goal can seem very overwhelming without a plan in place. It can consume you like it did me. Whatever your goal may be you must have some type of plan to help you be successful.

You must believe that the plan will get you to your goal and then do the plan to the best of your ability. In this particular case, even though I am in the field of fitness and strength and conditioning, I knew there was a more qualified expert to give me a better chance to succeed.

To sum up:
- Find your goal.
- Have an expert develop a plan for you.
- Turn your thoughts of doubt into energy for the task ahead.
- Follow that plan to the absolute best of your ability.

The training

Training for SEALFIT was filled with things that seemed crazy at the time. My workouts were long. I hated dedicating that much time to my own training (Sometimes two hours a day), but I knew in the end I would be able to help more people achieve their goals if I put myself through this test.

Here are a few of the workouts I did to prep for SEALFIT.

Workout 1

- 5K with 35-pound rucksack and boots for time (going as hard as I could go—my goal was get my heart rate as high as possible, which told me I was pushing it)
- Rest five minutes
- Repeat

Workout 2 –Murph in under 60 minutes (I'll explain about Murph later)

- One-mile run
- 100 pull-ups
- 200 push-ups
- 300 squats
- One-mile run

The thought of doing some of these workouts again makes me a little sick, but what allowed me to train this way for four months was a goal and the support from my team.

There was an endpoint. I knew I needed to be in the best shape of my life by September 15, the date of the SEALFIT training. I also knew I had six other buddies who were working hard to prepare, and I did not want to let them down.

Many times I would drive to the Jersey Shore and train with a few of my buddies who were also preparing for SEALFIT. This got me used to running on the sand, especially when I had to wear the boots. I always trained better when I had them with me. Training alone is very challenging.

Results are achieved when you set a goal and you have support along the way. We posted our training every night, and if someone went a few days without training, they were held accountable by the others in the group.

These two things are essential to have success:

1. A goal
2. Social support

I had both of these and it helped tremendously when I had to perform workouts like the ones above.

Find your goal.

What do you want to accomplish?

- If you want to lose fat then you MUST test your body fat percentage and set a specific date when you want to drop that number and by how much.
- If you want to make the varsity squad next year, then you better improve your mindset, athleticism, nutrition, and your sport-specific skills between now and then to put yourself in a position to succeed.
- Find another athlete who was on the varsity squad last year and train with him. Put yourself in a position where you are constantly surrounded by people better then you.
- Write your goals down.
- Google SMART goals to help you get more specific.
- Find people you trust and tell them about what you want to accomplish, ask them to support you.
-

Success is around the corner! We just need to identify when we will know when we have it.

Two days before ...

When SEALFIT was just two days away, I found myself excited

and nervous. There were many thoughts running through my head, not all of them with the right mindset.

I keep going back and forth from the Growth to the Fixed Mindset. One minute I would be feeling proud of all the work I had done over the last three months. The next, I would have this empty, nervous feeling that I was not prepared.

Some days I would drop down and do 10 pushups, and it would feel like I was back at day one. Other days I would drop down and feel like I could bang out 50.

Physically, I know I am not back at day one, and the ONLY thing that would bring me back to that is if I believe that.

If my Fixed Mindset questions that I am not ready, I will not be ready.

If my Growth Mindset tells me I am proud of all the work I have done and I am going to do the best that I can, I will be ready.

The power of team

As part of getting ready, I noticed the *power of team*.

The other day I asked the GFP team to train with me for my final workout. We had eight hill sprints up a nearby street. Many of my friends saw us out there. I woke up that day tired and not feeling good about the workout, but after Tom, Joe, Michelle, Chris, and Bern all agreed to run with me, I had this surge of energy.

We all ran together and it was tough, but in the end I felt great about my last workout because they pushed me to get the most out of it.

I know from what I have heard that SEALFIT is about being a team and staying together, leaving no one behind. It is not an individual competition.

This is true in all of our lives. Most of us are part of some kind of team. It could be family, a sports team, a church group, a Mastermind group, or something else. A strong bond in a group brings your performance to a higher level, especially when there is trust between the members of the group.

Right before the SEALFIT day, I had two thoughts about the Growth Mindset:

- Trust you have done your best and avoid worrying about whether you could have done better.
- Surround yourself with people that will bring the best out in you and vice versa.

SEALFIT arrives ... and no hands on hips!

The start of SEALFIT was a bit of a shocker. Normally when we train, there is a period of some foam rolling, stretching, some mobility work, and so forth—that is, some kind of warm-up period.

At 5:59 a.m., all of a sudden, our instructors QD and Brad, both former Navy SEALs, flipped a switch and were screaming in our faces, making us do pushups and running around like crazy men. Then QD told us we MUST stay within six feet of him at all times. He takes off sprinting down the streets of Avon—none of us were within 50 yards of him—he could fly.

At 6:02 a.m., I found myself more out of breath than I have ever been before from trying to stay within six feet of QD. It was barely possible. I knew at that moment that this would be the most challenging day of my life.

He would run back, holler at us for how out of shape we were, and then do it all over again.

By 6:10 a.m., we had probably run 20 long sprints and done about 100 pushups. We were in for a long day. At that point, he kept saying, "Only 11 hours and 50 minutes left!" It was demoralizing.

One of our biggest challenges was not placing our hands on our hips when we were tired. Placing your hands on your hips is a position of rest, and in the SEALs, it is a position of weakness. I was the first one to get nailed, and the punishment for this is leading your team through a set of no-handed burpees on the concrete.

No-handed burpees on the concrete is pure punishment, and I am definitely shocked no one broke their nose or ribs.

Then I got caught again a few minutes later. It is the worst feeling in the world when your own personal lack of discipline causes your teammates to suffer. I felt awful.

They were trying to teach us discipline. A lack of discipline gets you no-handed burpees during your workout, but with the SEALs, a lack of discipline could mean getting killed or you getting someone else killed.

I started to stand at attention with my hands out to the side about a foot away from my hips so there was no possible way I could rest my hands on them. It burned my shoulders to stand this way, but there was no way I was going to put my team through another set of no-handed burpees.

Many other guys got nailed after me and we all started to stand like that. We got much better as the day went on and our discipline improved.

The lesson from this is to display discipline in your own life.

There is no better example than to model a Navy SEAL. To become a SEAL, you must have extreme discipline. Their incredible discipline is one of the reasons why the Navy SEALs are the best in the world at what they do.

Discipline is not easy, but many times we will have to suffer through pain in order to learn lessons of change. Embrace this pain, learn from it, and move forward toward a more disciplined life.

Ten minutes into it

Ten minutes into it. Eleven hours and 50 minutes to go. One thing at a time.

I talked about the first 10 minutes of SEALFIT being absolutely exhausting. We probably sprinted as fast as we could over a mile and performed a ton of pushups. It was like this huge wave just came and crushed us.

I also told about QD, and how demoralizing it was that he kept telling us there were only 11 hours and 50 minutes left. To think that we had to move our bodies for that much more time and to realize how exhausted we already were was very tough.

This happens in our own lives. When we think about all the things we have to do, it can get overwhelming. That's why we need to *take one thing at a time.*

At SEALFIT, there were countless different activities we did throughout the 12-plus-hour period. The only thing we could do was our best, one thing at time. The more we thought about what was next or when it would be over, the tougher it got.

Hopefully you have some type of calendar or to-do list that you work off of daily. Do not get overwhelmed by how much you have to do. Simply take what is the absolute most important thing to your life and get it done.

At SEALFIT, the most important thing was the current task.

Always remember to prioritize in your life what is most important.

Your time is your most precious commodity.

Take one thing at a time, and do it great. Always remember that the things that are most important to your life deserve your absolute best.

The log

One of the most challenging parts of SEALFIT was the log. The log weighed about 200 pounds. Even today, the thought of it today really makes me sick.

We started with the log about half-a-mile from the beach. The plan was to teach us (very briefly) how to pick the log up as a team and walk with it. We had to arrange the height so the tallest person was in the back. I felt so bad for Uncle Mike, who was always in front and definitely got the worst of the log. Uncle Mike is the strongest individual I know.

While walking the log to the beach, it was very bumpy at first. I kept walking into the guy in front of me but we had to find a way to keep moving forward. We finally found that we needed to carry the log at an angle. It got much easier.

We carried the log all the way to the beach, where we expected a little break. There was none. For the next 90 minutes, we trained with the log—pressing it over our heads and our faces, going in the water with the log, sit-ups with the log, races against the clock with the log, holding the log on our chest—it was brutal.

The log was the ultimate symbol of teamwork. It was impossible for one man to lift the log. We had to learn very quickly to work together and communicate as a team. We got much better as the day went on.

There were even times where we found out how to use the water to help us. When doing sit-ups with the log, each one took an absolute max effort from each of us. All of a sudden one was easy.

We started to time our sit-ups for when the wave came, which made it much easier.

The log signified problem solving and communication at its finest. After we finished with the log, we started to do other things without it. I glanced over at the wet, sandy log and thought, "Oh, man, we have to still have to bring that thing a half-mile back." I know all the other guys thought the same thing.

Finally, twelve-and-a-half hours into our training, as the sun was going down, we grabbed the log and started training with it again. We started towards the street from the beach, and on the way up, we heard the words "SEALFIT mission, you are dismissed."

We carried the log to a truck waiting for it to take it back. It was an amazing way to end it.

Families, sports teams, and businesses all need teamwork and communication. If there are some people going one way and others going another, success will be very hard to attain. Each person needs to put the team before themselves in order for this to work. If while I was holding the log over my face and I let go, it would have crushed the other guys holding the log.

Find things you can do with your family, team, or business to build strength as a team. These exercises we went through were lessons that will last a lifetime, and I know we will all be better team players and communicators going forward.

My suggestion: Find something other than the log. ☺

The 20-times factor

One of the purposes of SEALFIT was to help you realize your true potential. Not only your potential for the physical, but for the mental as well.

During training for SEALFIT, I got olecranon bursitis. The inflammation caused my elbow to blow up like a balloon. Push-ups and pull-ups are a huge part of SEALFIT. There are minimum requirements just to be able to participate.

Because of my elbow, I had to drastically cut the number of push-ups and pull-ups I was doing in training. This was my weak point going in, so I was very concerned.

During the 12-plus hours of training, there were many times when I thought to myself, I am close to done.

We trained for about seven hours and then did a workout called Murph. Murph is a workout named after Michael Murphy, who bravely died for his country.

This is Murph—and yes, we had to wear our 23-pound pack during the entire workout:

- One-mile run
- 100 pull-ups
- 200 push-ups
- 300 squats
- One-mile run

On my first mile, all I kept thinking about was the 100 pull-ups and 200 push-ups. Would the elbow hold up? Oh, yeah, they told us to shoot for under an hour, so now it was looking crazy. We were already shot from the previous seven hours of training.

I finished the first mile and started on the pull-ups. Every time we would finish a round of five pull-ups, 10 push-ups, and 15 squats, they would give me a chalk mark. I needed 20 of these chalk marks to start the final mile.

It felt like there was about an hour between each chalk mark. The trainer kept saying, "I'm bored, Vinny, let me write something down."

He was watching me like a hawk. If I didn't do a full Navy SEAL push-up (chest to floor and full lock-out) it didn't count. If my squat was not low enough, it didn't count. This was tough.

After what felt like an eternity, I started the last mile and finished Murph. I was shot.

After Murph, we had a 30-minute lunch break. I had brought no food other than a CLIF bar and two peaches, the only things I ate all day.

We started back up at 2 p.m. and went all the way to 6:30 p.m. I thought I was done after Murph. If you asked me at the time if I could train for four more hours after Murph, I would have said no way.

Something kept me going. It was the team, the coaches, and the new lessons I was learning about having 20 times more than you think.

I will cherish this lesson forever in my life. I realized that what I think is my best is not really my best. I have more, you have more.

We can all do so much better than we tell ourselves. We just have to find a way to bring it out. But it is there. This day taught me that, and this lesson will be with me forever.

You have 20 times what you think you have.

Determination

SEALFIT was the most grueling 12 hours of physical work we had ever endured. Not only was it physical but it was mental, very mental.

We were told to do things that none of us would ever ask a paying client to do. There were times when we were looking at each other with looks that said, "Is this really happening?"

Here are a few of the crazy things we experienced:

- No-handed burpees on the concrete
- On our backs, heads in the water, waves crashing, while holding a 200-pound log over our faces
- Dragging us backward while our faces dragged in the sand, and no, we could not turn our heads, nose, eyes, or mouth in the sand

Despite all the mental challenges, we were lasting through the physical. The biggest issue holding us back during the physical challenge was cramping. One of our buddies was cramping so bad that he was screaming at the top of his lungs. I have never heard a grown, very strong man scream like this. His body was frozen, his arms would not move. His legs would not bend.

He continued.

After the main cramping subsided, he started to run. It was slower than a slow walk, but he was running. His legs would not bend, and his body was stiffer than I have ever seen another human being that was not dead.

He continued.

He was determined not to quit because he would NOT let us down. He was focused on the team and all we had accomplished that day, and he gave every ounce of everything he had to keep going.

This was an ultimate display of determination.

I cannot begin to express to all of you what a life-changing experience this was for me.

Attack your week with determination. Do not give up. DO everything you can to accomplish what you want. You have so much more in the tank than you realize—you just have to find it.

CHAPTER 8: HEALTH & FITNESS LESSONS

As you can see, SEALFIT changed my life in a huge way and taught me many lessons. Here are some of my other thoughts about health and fitness that I think are really important.

Be a good example to your children

A while back, several members of my team and I attended a conference in Providence. The keynote speaker was two-time Super Bowl-winning coach Dick Vermeil. Since all of us are football guys, we were very excited to hear him speak.

He spoke for an hour and had several great points, but the one I want to highlight today is to *be a good example*. Be the example of discipline for your children. There is a great chance that if you as parents live a healthy life, then your children will do the same.

One of our goals is to help the kids and adults in this community live healthy happy lives. We cannot accomplish this ourselves. We only have a few hours a week. We need help from the parents out there. We need you to be the model. It starts with you.

But … Here is the problem that most of you have come to me with: "My kids never listen to me. I tell them what to do all the time and they just do not listen."

I am going to suggest you try an approach that I am sure will work—maybe not right away, but eventually it will kick in.

Be the model of discipline with your health for your children.

- Eat clean 90 percent of the time

- Exercise three to five days per week
- Get good sleep

Take care of your body. It is not selfish to be healthy, and your children have a much better chance to be healthy themselves if you are.

My advice is less talk, more action. Be the good example.

Fat loss and willpower

So what's this about eating clean 90 percent of the time? If you have trouble with willpower and the food you eat, be sure to adopt the "90 percent rule."

The 90 percent rule gives you strategic times throughout the week to break your willpower but will not hurt you in your fat loss quest. If you eat 21 meals in a week, 2 of them should be not within the guidelines of your fat loss meal plan. Enjoy!

Eat clean 90 percent of the time and you are good to go.

Exercise and willpower

Exercise has been called Miracle-Gro for the brain, according to Harvard researcher John Ratey, who wrote a great book called *Spark: The Revolutionary New Science and the Brain.*

"Exercise in many ways optimizes your brain to learn," says Dr. John Ratey, a clinical associate professor of psychiatry at Harvard Medical School in Boston, who's at work on a book about exercise and the brain.

Exercise improves circulation throughout the body, including the brain,

Ratey explains.

Exercise also boosts metabolism, decreases stress, and improves mood and attention, all of which help the brain perform better, he says.

"The brain cells actually become more resilient and more pliable and are more ready to link up," he says.

It's this linking up that allows us to retain new information.

Obviously, we help people exercise for a living, so you know we are a huge fan of the health benefits, but I never really knew how good it actually was for our brains until digging a little deeper.

What you need to know

Exercise strengthens the pre-frontal cortex of the brain. A healthy pre-frontal cortex, the part of the brain that is responsible for decision-making and regulating behavior, will give you more willpower.

The more willpower you have, the greater the success you will achieve.

What is optimal?

- Two to three days of strength training (30 to 60 minutes)
- Two to three days of cardiovascular training (30 to 90 minutes)

I say this often: Training two times per week is the bare minimum. Results across the board will improve dramatically when a three- to five-day training program is incorporated.

Now you have a reason other than general health and fat loss to exercise more. It's your brain, the most advanced organ in the world—treat it well.

Derek: An inspiring visit

Recently, I received a visit from the nephew of one of our GFP clients. He was visiting from Minnesota and wanted to stop by and check out GFP. We knew he was coming and we were very excited to meet him because there was something extremely special about this young man.

He was a U.S. Army veteran, actually a wounded warrior. When I think of an Army vet or wounded warrior, I usually picture a guy in his 60s that fought in Vietnam.

Not this kid. He was 27 years old.

He walked in and Big Tom showed him around the gym. You could tell by the look on his face how excited he was to see our facility. He loved the turf, the chains, and the minimal equipment we had in our gym. Just like it should be, he said.

I sat with him, and we talked for almost two hours. He wanted to start his own gym back in Minnesota. I worked with him to help develop a plan to get things rolling and we got to talking about his leg.

When he was 23 years old, he led a team into a house in Baghdad, Iraq, and was shot in the knee. For almost five years, he lived with a leg that simply did not work. This did not stop him from doing things like running tough mudders and still working out like a mad man.

He finally pleaded with the doctors to amputate his leg. He now has a prosthetic leg. The doctors are getting mad at him because he is so active that they have to replace parts on his prosthetic way more frequently than normal.

He trains harder than ever. This guy squats 275 with a prosthetic leg!

Imagine feeling sorry for yourself in the gym and then looking over at the guy with one leg working his tail off. Incredible! He is such an inspiration to me and I hope this story inspires you too. I know his gym will be successful, and I am making it my mission to make sure it is—my small contribution to a guy that sacrificed so much for our freedom.

I believe his story alone will make him a success. No one that trains at his gym will ever be able to say "I can't do it" or "It's too hard." There is built-in motivation from the story of a brave young man that gave so much.

Good luck, Derek. The GFP family is fully behind you. Thank you for all you have done and thank for the motivation to tell us that nothing is out of our reach.

Seeing your goals through to the end

People are always very enthusiastic about new goals! They put a lot of energy into beginning a new program or setting out on a new path.

Isn't that how it always starts?

Isn't that what everyone does?

You set goals or resolutions, say for instance at the start of the new year, and then do great for the first few weeks. Then that discipline simply seems to fade away and you are right back where you started.

Not you. Not now. And here's why.

The first step for any goal is finding out what you want to accomplish, what is it you are truly going after. It can't just be "eat better" and "exercise more." It needs to something tangible. Something you can measure.

Maybe your goal is to work out three days a weeks instead of two. This is simple:

- Two workouts a week is 104 per year (last year)
- Three workouts a week is 156 per year (your goal)

You can break this down into smaller chunks as well:

- 156 workouts a year is 13 per month

So you need to work out 13 times a month to achieve this goal. If there are four days left in the month and you have only done eight workouts, what you need to do? Work out every day for the next four days!

Would you have done that last year? No way!

Now with this measured goal of 156, you will turn on the heat and make sure you accomplish it. This is a goal that you can measure.

Once you find your goal, how do you stay accountable to it?

Simple. Look at it every day and have it on you at all times.

I have many of our clients write their goal on a business card and keep it in their wallet so they can see it every day. Many people just like you are starting to get off on the right foot. The difference is that some people are armed with what they want to accomplish and have it handwritten on a card in their wallet. This means they are 90 percent more likely to achieve their goal.

Moving your health to the front of the line

I am going to come clean and admit failure. I was not doing the things I need to do to perform at my highest level.

Here was the situation.

I was waking up every morning with pain in my ankle, the same area where I broke my leg more than 12 years ago. It was affecting me in my work life and in my drive to exercise and train. Over time, it got worse and worse to the point where I had to walk down the steps in the morning one at a time.

I believe what happened was that after I broke my leg the bone healed, but I been compensating for so long to stay away from my ankle that I developed tightness and weakness in other places.

Soon after I healed, I started a very vigorous running program and I believe that reinforced bad mechanics. It was not until recently that it came full circle and started affecting my life. My body ran out of compensations.

People were even asking me if I was limping, and I definitely was. I had not injured it again; it was just an old injury that I never took proper care of after it happened. I knew what I needed to do. And this moved it to one of the highest things on my priority list.

I knew I had a ton of scar tissue in that area that needed to be broken up. Whenever there is an injury like this, the body will heal itself and create scar tissue. It is hard for blood to run through this scar tissue, and it limits range of motion. This is the body's natural way of healing but it can cause a host of problems if not addressed properly.

I went to a massage therapist in New Providence who worked on my ankle. It was very painful, but I knew I needed to get this done. I got six hours of massage over a period of three weeks. It helped tremendously.

I started walking every morning to help rush the blood flow to the area and heal it. I worked with a great therapist, Michelle, and she did fascial stretch therapy (FST) on it a bunch of times.

The lesson here is this:

- *Pain limits us in many ways.* When we are in pain, no matter what it is, it dramatically decreases our quality of life. Pain decreases motivation to exercise, it compromises your mindset, and it affects your life with work and family.
- *Old injuries can cause new problems.* Take care of any injuries when they occur. Regularly use massage and FST to help

prevent problems down the road.

- *Take action.* Getting a two-hour massage in the middle of the day was torture for me. I knew there were so many other things I should have been doing, but I forced myself to do it because I knew that my health was a top priority to help me be more successful in the future.
- *Regular treatment for your body.* I will now be getting a massage every week and get a stretch with Michelle every week because I know it will keep me healthy for the long haul.

Purpose and losing fat

The majority of the time, people come to us and say, "I need to lose 10 pounds." This is fine but there is a problem here.

What happens when they achieve this goal? Are they satisfied? Usually, no. It is normally replaced with another goal of losing five more pounds, and so on.

The issue here is that we are linking the loss of weight with our success and not linking having a healthy body with our true purpose in our life.

Here is why I strive to follow the GFP Pyramid (mindset, eat clean, train smart, recover):

- To live a long healthy life with my family
- To set a great example for my children and family members
- To have energy so I can be more productive and become more successful
- To live life without pain

I do not work out to lose weight, nor do I work out to impress others with my strength or muscle mass.

I do not work out to fit into better clothes or to be able to eat bad food.

My fitness and nutrition are directly linked to my purpose in life. When my purpose is being fulfilled I am happy. Being happy is essentially the ultimate goal in life. My purpose is to provide a happy life for my family through changing the lives of the people who train and work at GFP.

Being in shape fuels this purpose.

- When I am not diligently eating well and exercising, my purpose is compromised.
- When I do not regularly, get a massage, or stretch, my purpose is compromised.
- When I do not get enough sleep, my purpose is compromised.
- When I do not practice the Growth Mindset, my purpose is compromised

This happens to me at times, and it is because I lose sight of why my health is so important. When this happens, I am letting down the people who depend on me. I am letting down my wife, my children, my team and all of you.

I have a responsibility to all these people to be healthy. This is why I strive to live by the GFP Pyramid. When we link our fitness goals with a percentage of body fat or weight loss, we can achieve them, but then this just creates another similar goal. It is fine to have these goals, but linking your happiness to a specific number is a recipe for chasing your tail.

Come up with your purpose in life, ask yourself how the GFP Pyramid fits into that purpose, and strive to use mindset, exercise, nutrition, and recovery to help you live your true purpose.

Vince's fitness jumpstart

I will admit that having two children took a toll on me. Vanessa and I had two girls in a span of 16 months, and although it is the most powerful thing that has ever happened to me, my health suffered.

I was in pain and fatigued because I was not living my life by the pyramid (the one we created!).

At one point, I thought I was a hypocrite because here I was telling people to be healthy and fit, and I was struggling with my own health and fitness. I truly took a serious look at the pyramid and said to myself, "You are not living your life by that pyramid."

My sleep was not normal and that was something that was difficult to change, having two babies in the house. This affected my energy and desire to exercise. When I did train, it was appalling and I would barely break a sweat because I was in pain and just tired.

As I mentioned before, old injuries started to flare up, and I found myself walking down the stairs very differently. I actually told myself I was walking down the stairs one at a time because I didn't want to wake the baby, but the reality was I HAD to walk down one step at time. It was my breaking point.

I needed a jump start. I needed a full commitment to moving my health to the front of the line.

- I made sure I had enough food for the day and I prioritized getting my meals in.
- I scheduled time for my workouts and actually changed the time. I used to work out around 2 p.m., so I moved it to 11:30 a.m. to make it more of a priority.
- I started a basic supplement schedule of the essentials: a multi-vitamin, fish oil, magnesium and greens drink. (And yes, GFP sells all of this. I only sell what I would take myself or give to my family.)
- Finally, I dedicated myself to stretching and massage. I scheduled one appointment each week and have done it consistently.

I cannot tell you the difference I feel. I feel like a new man. I pop out of bed in the morning. I am getting more and better work done. I have less stress and I have much more energy to play with my daughters (the main reason I work out).

I am not perfect. I have been where you may be and I know exactly what to do to get out of it.

Progress, not perfection

One of my best friends, Paul Reddick, teaches this as one of the main principles in his seminar. I have this hammered into my head, and every time I think I should be farther along, I quickly reflect on the progress that I've made.

This is really all that matters—are we making progress?

There was a young man in our gym recently that struggled with jumping rope. He had never done it on his life and he was not able to get even one jump.

The other day he was getting three to five jumps in a row.

Progress, not perfection.

He is not YET good at jumping rope, but he was much better than he was a few days before. If he continues to jump rope, he will continue to make progress.

When you get halfway up the mountain, you can look at how far you have to go or you can focus on how far you have come.

Progress, not perfection.

In my princess-driven world right now, there is Ariel, Merida, Sleeping Beauty and Snow White all over my house. One of the lines from the movie *Brave* is, "A princess strives for perfection."

I changed this and told Bella a princess strives for *progress, not perfection.*

I am going to throw that DVD out.

If you have a goal of losing fat, and you only lose 1.5 pounds of fat in a month, many would get frustrated. If you lost 1.5 pounds of fat every month for 12 months, that is 18 pounds of fat. I will guarantee satisfaction if you do it for 12 months in a row!

Progress, not perfection.

CHAPTER 9: WHAT IS CHARACTER?

In these last few chapters, I want to share with you many of the lessons I've learned and that I hope will help us all continue to grow. These lessons involve character—character in ourselves and our children, especially in their performance as students and athletes, but as human beings as well. These lessons involve having a strong Growth Mindset, being grateful, helping others. I hope that the things I have learned can help you and your loved ones live a happier, more successful life.

Vince's favorite quote of all time

We can come back from almost any failure, although some are harder than others. This is where priorities come into our lives. We must do the work on the front end to make sure the most important things in our lives stay most important.

I rarely get struck by a quote, but this one is going up in my house and I will read it every day.

Before you read it, may I ask one favor? Forward this quote to a friend who needs to read this.

Here is arguably my favorite quote of all time:

"Imagine life is a game in which you are juggling five balls.

The balls are called work, family, health, friends, and integrity.

And you're keeping all of them in the air.

But one day you finally come to understand that work is a rubber ball.

If you drop it, it will bounce back.

The other four balls are made of glass.

If you drop one of these, it will be irrevocably scuffed, nicked, perhaps even shattered.

And once you truly understand the lesson of the five balls, you will have the beginnings of balance in your life."

— James Patterson

The power of having a purpose

The James Patterson quote above is one of the most powerful I know. Here's another quote that carries a lot of meaning for me:

> **"The value of a life is always measured by how much you give away."**

This quote is from Pastor Andy Stanley.

Being a deep thinker and always looking at the big picture has brought me to great place of clarity. I am clear that every day on this earth I am striving to leave my mark on as many people as possible. This could be through writing, speaking, training, coaching, or leading, but it all leads to the main purpose of my life.

Knowing my purpose has enabled me to truly understand what the most important things in life really are.

Answering this question gave me the perspective.

How do you want to be remembered?

Answering this question gave me the insight to write my purpose statement:

To be remembered as a man of character that transformed countless lives and inspired others to the same.

This statement drives me to live my life in a way that will fulfill this purpose. What I read, the seminars I attend, who I hang out with, the work I do, and how I decide to invest my time all come back to this.

So when you are bogged down by the grind of life, take a step back and answer this question. It will not make every problem in your life disappear; it will just enable you to think about them differently:

How do you want to be remembered?

The first pillar of character: Honesty

Parents? Do your kids have character?

If I were to ask this question to most people, they would say yeah, yeah, I have good character. But do we even know what having good character is?

Before we go deeper into character, we must understand that character is to be looked at with the Growth Mindset. Character is NOT set and can be improved. After reading in length about what it means to have good character, I came across four pillars that if lived, demonstrate having great character.

The pillar that always came up as number one: *Honesty*

Honesty is always the quality that is selected first among great leaders who demonstrate high character. If you strive to do great things in your life, being honest is a quality you MUST display. It is very difficult to be a person of character if you are not honest because it is the number one virtue for having good character.

So before you begin to tell a small lie to get you out of trouble or simply shift a story around, remember that every time dishonesty comes out of you, it is a strike against your character. There is not a person in the world that wants to have bad character, but we must work towards it.

Life will challenge us to have bad character, so the decisions we make must be made with this in mind. It is important to have these virtues in place so we make the right decisions in our lives and are thought of by others as having good character.

But more importantly, you needs to know that you strive to have the best character you can. Being honest is the start.

The second pillar of character: Respect

Are you a bully?

I remember when I was a freshman and my sister was a senior. I looked at some of the guys in her class as gods, not because they were good at football or were big and strong, but because they respected me, acknowledged me, simply said hello to me. I still think very highly of those guys today.

The second trait of great character is respect.

It is obvious that we as parents strive to instill the quality of respect in our children. Respect needs to be given to all, especially your peers.

There is something called the Golden Rule and it states: People matter.

If we adopt the mindset that our focus is to make all those around us feel better, then we will affect the lives of many.

I hear too many stories of kids not respecting other kids. This needs to change.

Students! You have the opportunity to be a plus or a minus in the lives of others.

Adopt the mindset that you will be a plus in the lives of your peers.

This especially goes for older high school students. This is your first opportunity in your life to be a leader, you have the opportunity simply because of your situation.

How do you handle this? Do you abuse it? Do you enforce your power, intimidate other kids, ignore situations where you can help?

Or do you become a role model that leads by example and respects everyone, helps people in need, and makes others feel good?

At school, this goes for teachers, faculty, janitors, lunch workers, crossing guards, peers, younger students—everyone you encounter in your day.

Think about this through your life as a young person:

- Am I a plus or a minus in the lives of my peers?
- Will that person remember me as a good person who respected me or as a bully?
- What can I do today to make someone feel better?

If you are a minus in the lives of others, if you do not respect them, and if you continually make people feel worse, the Growth Mindset says you can improve all this.

Do not dwell on your past, focus on doing the right thing in the future.

The third pillar of character: Responsibility

- Do what you are supposed to do
- Plan ahead
- Persevere: keep on trying!
- Always do your best
- Use self-control
- Be self-disciplined
- Think before you act
- Consider the consequences
- Be accountable for your words, actions, and attitudes
- Set a good example for others

The third pillar of character is responsibility.

Let's start with the negative side of this word and talk about irresponsibility. If you are irresponsible, you do not use self-control, do not set a good example for others, do not plan ahead, and do not display self-discipline.

I know that no one wants to be labeled as irresponsible, but if we continually forget things, are late, and do not plan our lives in advance, it will come out as a knock on our character. I am sure there are plenty of great people out there who are simply very irresponsible and get labeled as people with weak character.

We need to be in control of our lives. We need to be responsible.

Action steps to being responsible:

- Be on time
- Do the things you say you will do
- Set a good example for others
- Think before you speak
- Plan your day ahead of time

The fourth pillar of character: Fairness

The fourth pillar of great character is fairness. Being fair means to play by the rules, be open minded, and not blame other people.

Fair play is always a positive. When I go out to see our athletes play, I root for them to play the best they ever have. More importantly I hope they carry themselves on the field with dignity, play by the rules, and respect their opponents.

If I attend a game where one of our athletes scores four touchdowns but has two personal fouls, I would not consider that a great game. A great game is performing the best you possibly can be while at the same time walking off the field knowing you respected your opponent, helped your teammates improve, and made your coaches proud to have you on their team.

The old saying that goes, "If you ain't cheating, you ain't trying," is not what I would consider a high-character quote.

One of the things I love about training athletes from different towns is that they get to know each other. Many athletes train with us in the same time slot in the summer and then play against each other in the fall. It is always great to see them play against each other because they have built a friendly rivalry in the gym and now take that to the field. We love to watch them interact and it has always been fair.

Athletes

- Do you respect your opponents, teammates, coaches, officials?
- Do you play by the rules?
- Do you help your teammates improve?
- Do you pick a teammate up when they make a mistake or do you bring them down further?

Your performance is measured by wins and losses, goals scored, and other similar factors, but your character is measured by how you act on the field.

The best athletes are the ones that do both.

The fifth pillar of character: Community

The final pillar of having great character is citizenship.

I am always very impressed with the amount of time our adult fitness clients spend in the community.

Many of the people that train at GFP are coaches, youth commissioners, or PTA members; they run silent auctions; or they act as members of town council or Board of Education presidents.

None of these are glorious, high-paying positions and take a lot of time and energy. I commend all of you for volunteering your time and making our community a better place for our children. You are all setting a great example for your children by demonstrating the final pillar of great character, citizenship.

I saw many examples of great citizenship during Hurricane Sandy. People came out of the woodwork to help others in need. I heard many stories of kids and adults stepping up and demonstrating great citizenship during this time.

Make it a priority to always be a great citizen, not just during times of crisis; great character is displayed all the time.

- Be involved in your community and strive to make it a better place
- When you are of age, vote.
- Be a good neighbor.
- *Drive safely! (This means you, high school kids!)*
- Respect authority.
- Protect the environment: recycle, clean up after yourself and your pets, live sustainably.
- Volunteer your time.

My challenge to my readers is to lead by example. Become the model for great character for your peers.

I am especially talking to older high school students. Like I have mentioned, you have been given a platform to be a role model and a leader simply because of your situation. Whether you know it or not, there is a freshman who thinks you are awesome. That young person will model themselves after you. Set this kid on the path to greatness and solid character. It is your time to step up, be the model for spreading character and greatness into the lives of others.

CHAPTER 10: BECOMING

This chapter is designed to give you some tips on getting better … no matter what you try, no matter what your goals, you can always get better. Take a look at some of these life lessons and try to become … whatever you want to be.

Three ways to become better … at everything

If students want to improve at their respective sports or activities, they must do a little more. Showing up and participating is fine, but if you expect to be competitive and be better tomorrow than you are today, work must be done.

There are no magic bullets that will all of a sudden turn an average player of student into great. There are, however, keystone habits that need to be acquired to become better every day.

- *Consistency.* One of the reasons we do not sell packages of sessions for our young athletes is because we want them to learn the habit of consistency. If an athlete buys a package of sessions to improve athleticism, strength, and speed, and they are given the freedom to use those sessions as they please, this does make it easy on their schedule but does not teach lessons of consistency.

  It may take 12 weeks to get eight workouts in, and this is not a way to improve or teach consistency or achieve the results your desire from training. For example if you are on three travel teams, have a math tutor , go to music class, do speed training, and have a ton of homework on top of all that, it is going to be very difficult to excel in all of these things.

There is simply too much or too little time and stimulus in each of these activities to get the full advantage. I do feel it is beneficial to participate in a broad variety of activities, but spreading kids so thin makes it hard for them to see a true benefit.

One of the reasons we see great results with our athletes is because they are put on a consistent schedule. If they adhere, they learn consistency and get excellent results.

- *Commitment.* When a kid commits to something, her or she will get excellent results. When I was in elementary school I hated playing trumpet. I was not committed to it. I practiced, but with a chip on my shoulder, and I even got special lessons to improve. but I remained a poor trumpet player because I simply was not committed to it.

This goes to show that you can still go through the motions and do a lot of stuff, but without commitment, life lessons are lost and results are minimal.

On the contrary, when I was in high school I was strongly committed to improving my SAT scores. I knew if I did not get them up, I would have had a tough time getting into the college I wanted. I was committed, and through many hours of SAT prep classes, I improved.

During the school year, we require a minimum commitment

of 12 weeks for our young athletes. We do not offer packages of sessions because our mission is to help improve the lives of our athletes. Teaching them lessons of commitment at a young age will develop more determination and grit later in life.

Making a commitment is harder and more time consuming but the lesson learned and the results achieved are worth it.

Shane Haddad (100-win wrestler) and Cassandra Squeri (1,000-point scorer), both area sports stars, have committed to year-round consistent general and specific training for more than five years.

- *Effort.* The third part of this success triangle is effort. We have had many athletes be committed to a program, consistent with their attendance, but when little effort is given, results are minimal. Lack of effort in anything will yield poor results.

Effort is a skill, largely determined by inner and outer motivation. As coaches, we individually motivate each athlete so he or she puts forth their best effort in the gym and strive for this to extend to all areas of their lives. We will always reward athletes for demonstrating great effort because we value effort much more than actual results or talent.

When a child puts forth a good effort. regardless of the result, praise is strongly encouraged. If my daughter brings home all C's and I know she put her best effort forward, I will be more than proud of her and will be sure to express this to her.

Our mission is to improve the quality of life for all the young people that come through our doors. We structure our program to have built-in life lessons of consistency, commitment, and effort. We take great pride in being the second voice of success in the lives of your children.

Two drills for success and happiness in two minutes

It is no secret that two things we want more of in our lives are success and happiness.

Try these three drills that take two minutes each to be happier and more successful.

- Smile.

There is nothing that brings more positive energy to others than a great smile. Even when you talk on the phone, you should be smiling. Smiling changes the shape of your vocal chords and makes your voice sound happier.

Be aware of how much you smile this week. Make a point to smile more often, and I think you will be pleasantly surprised that your own happiness and the happiness of those around you will improve.

Two-Minute Drill

If you are having a rough day, look at yourself in the mirror and smile for two minutes straight. This will definitely change your mindset.

- Get things done

When you accomplish things that you want, your brain releases dopamine. This is a chemical that makes you happy when it is released. The best thing that you can do to get more done is to have a to-do list.

Write it in the AM and then cross things off when you accomplish them. I even like to write very small things down that take almost no time or effort, since this still gives your brain a release of dopamine and will keep you going strong throughout the week.

Two-Minute Drill

Set a timer for two minutes and write down the five things you want to accomplish today. Cross them off throughout the day, and you have a constant stream of dopamine being released. At the end of the day, crumple that paper and toss it because you crushed that to-do list.

- Body language

Be well aware of your body language and know that there has been research done that tells us how important good posture is to how we feel. Believe it or not, this is why we train the upper back as much as we do. When your posture is improved, it is easier to display better body language.

If you are constantly hunched forward due to weak or tight muscles. it is much harder to maintain good, open body language.

Two-Minute Drill

Want to feel better?

Stand up and put your feet shoulder-width apart. Put your arms out to the side and hold that position for two minutes. This anteater position is proven to increase testosterone levels and decrease cortisol.

Try it before you go into a meeting, do a presentation, play a game, or tackle any other important task.

Don't believe me?

Watch this video: http://www.ted.com/talks/amy_cuddy_your_body_language_shapes_who_you_are.html?quote=1924

Dance with your fears!

Last week I had an opportunity of a lifetime. I run a mastermind group with my friend Paul where we meet with 13 gym owners from around the country to help them build their gyms.

For our first meeting, we brought in a guest speaker: Seth Godin. Seth is probably one of the most well-known business and marketing authors in the world. He has written 17 books, including *The Dip: A Little Book that Teaches You When to Quit (And When to Stick)*, *Tribes: We Need You to Lead Us*, and *Purple Cow: Transform Your Business by Being Remarkable*.

We met with Seth at his private office in New York. It was probably not the crew he was used to working with. Normally he speaks for business guys, writers, or lawyers wearing sharp blue suits.

When 16 meatheads walked through the door wearing hoodies and yellow Bumblebee shirts, he was definitely taken aback.

The hour was the most impactful hour of learning I have done in my life.

He talked about entrepreneurship, culture, marketing, and growth, among many other topics.

He had a way of taking a very, very big idea and narrowing it down into one sentence.

Here is the one I think applies to each of you reading this today.

It's about fear. Fear comes from thinking about what might happen. We all have fear.

Don't deny fear—embrace it.

Forgive yourself for the fear.

Dance with your fear.

New Providence Senior Night

I was recently asked to speak at the New Providence High School Senior Athletic Awards dinner. It was a great honor to be asked to do this and I was very excited about the opportunity.

This was a very special night for me as many of these graduating seniors were some of the first ever athletes to train at GFP. Many of them started with us as eighth graders, and now they are going off to college. Amazing how time flies!

As I watched them get their recognition, I was so excited for each of them. Many will be playing a college sport as well, something I know will develop mindset, work ethic, and character.

I spoke briefly about three things last night.

- Focus on other people. Care.

Showing genuine care and concern for others is one of the most important skills in life. You develop strong relationships with people when you have their best interests at heart.

When you meet people, make great eye contact and shake hands firmly. During conversations, make that conversation as the most important one.

Remember people's names, and use their names. Even if it is a person just working at a store or a restaurant, use their name; they wear a nametag for a reason.

- *Find your passion, and make it your profession.*

I still feel like I have never had a job. Owning GFP is simply something I love to do. I love my craft, I love my team, I love our clients—there is nothing I would rather be doing. I see this as one of the most important keys to happiness in life.

If you have a job that *have to* go to versus one you *get to* go to, regardless of the financials, you may not live life to the fullest. I know some people that make a lot of money, hate their job, and are miserable.

My advice to these young people was to push hard to find their passion and go with it.

- Practice the Growth Mindset.

Many of these students will get cut from the team, fail tests, get fired, or break-up with a significant other over the next few years. The Growth Mindset teaches us that these incidents are learning experiences, nothing more. They are information to help us improve and be better next time.

The Fixed Mindset views these things as who we are. If we fail a math test, we stink at math. If we have a bad lacrosse game, we stink at lacrosse.

This is the mindset we need to avoid. Adopt the Growth Mindset, and the only possibility is to improve.

The strongest man I know

After years in the fitness industry, I have been around some very strong people. I have seen men bend steel bars with their bare hands, finish the Ironman triathlon, and deadlift 800 pounds—but there is one man at GFP that puts all of them to shame.

He puts them to shame with the courage and toughness he shows in his battle with pancreatic cancer.

My friend and long-time GFP client Carl D'Emilio has been fighting this disease for several months. Carl gave me his blessing to write about him because his battle has taught him so many lessons that he wants to share with others.

As painful as this battle is, he is still putting others first and looking for every opportunity to help us improve. He wanted to share how we can withstand so much more pain than we actually realize.

I see Carl regularly for lunch, along with a few other jokers (Tom and Jeanine), at something we call the Carl D Lunch Box. We meet to spend more time with Carl, but really we just talk about sports and life, and once in a while we talk about the fight.

After a long talk with Carl the other day, I asked him what he has learned during his battle with cancer. The big rock he kept coming back to was, "Live every day and fight every day."

Life has put a huge obstacle in front of him, and this is his mantra. He not going to let chemo knock him down and affect the time with his family. He's going to fight back.

He is going into it with the mindset that he will "kick cancer's ass." That is one thing he is definitely doing. He has stood face to face with this disease and is giving every ounce of fight he has.

He is fighting. He wants people to know that you can endure so much more than you think you can. He wants you to take your biggest problem you have today and TAKE IT HEAD ON!

Fight!

Get help too, because you can't do it alone. Carl has an army of family, friends, and doctors standing with him.

Whatever fight you are in stand in front of it, ACCEPT IT, AND TAKE IT ON!

None of us is facing the same battle as Carl. He doesn't wish this on anyone.

But—He does want you to take what it has taught him. He wants you to apply it to your life. Carl does not want sympathy, he wants action. He wants people to get better from his fight. He wants people to change through the strength he has demonstrated.

He wants you to FIGHT THROUGH IT ... and WIN.

One word that is the key to all success

The more I read about business, self-development, and parenting, the more this term comes up. When Vanessa and I were sitting down to create our Gabriele family core values, GRIT was one value that was non-negotiable.

We would understand GRIT, have GRIT ourselves, and do everything in our power to raise our daughters with GRIT.

GRIT: The perseverance and passion for a long-term goal.

Grit enables you to maintain your motivation over a long period of time despite experiences with failure and adversity. Grit is not subject to school, sports, or business. Having grit in all aspects of your life will help with better relationships, family life, fitness, health, and happiness.

I see grit in many of the girls I have trained that have torn their ACL. They work harder after this injury than they ever have in their lives. The ACL tear gave them more grit. The goal is getting back on the field; they almost develop this chip on their shoulder that nothing will stop them.

I often tell parents in consultations that this injury is tough but it is also a gift. Tearing your ACL is no picnic. It's an eight-to-twelve-month recovery process. But …

It takes your GRIT to the next level. This GRIT stays with you. A high school girl that has torn her ACL is better prepared for life.

Life will constantly challenge you, and your level of grit will determine your success. Continually overcoming struggles is the key to developing more GRIT. Every time you bounce back you strengthen your level of GRIT.

How you view failure is a key principle in developing GRIT. If you view failure as fuel for improvement, you will be in a better mindset to display GRIT. Many people just have more GRIT than others. The ones who will NOT develop more GRIT are the ones who believe that you are just born with it.

The people who believe you can improve your own personal level of GRIT are the ones who achieve true success.

What is your level of GRIT?

The Paul Reddick challenge

Many of you do not know who Paul is, but he happens to be a great friend of mine and a fellow SEALFIT finisher.

Paul is an incredible guy who is always putting others before himself. He continually offers help and shows a genuine interest in others and never asks for anything in return.

Paul created this challenge and now I am passing it on to you.

Here is the challenge:

- How much can you give to others this week?
- What special things can you do for your loved ones?
- Who needs Help? Who needs encouragement?
- What gifts need to be given?
- What favors need to be done?
- What words need to be said? Or NOT said?
- What compliments need to be given?

Record all that you do on your phone or in a note pad and keep a running tab.

How I learned to pay it forward

Before I opened GFP, I was a curious trainer.

There was a legendary coach named Mike Boyle from Boston whom I looked at as a mentor. I watched every DVD he had and read every book and article he wrote.

I had never met him, but I felt like I knew him. One day I decided to email him and ask for help.

Guess what? He answered all my questions!

Then, I asked if I could visit him in Boston and ask him a huge list of questions.

His one word response: "Absolutely!"

The meeting I had was life changing; it taught me so many lessons. I learned a lot about training. I learned a lot about running a fitness business. But most of all, I learned how to pay it forward.

Here was a legend in the industry taking two hours out of his day to help a young, inexperienced trainer. I am now in a position where I frequently get asked to help others. Whether it is a young aspiring trainer, a college kid seeking career advice, or even an executive looking to balance his or her life.

I keep finding myself in these positions, and I always help because that is what Coach Boyle did for me.

What I'm saying is that you have to step up for other people in your life. Maybe it's a friend, a co-worker, or even someone you do not know that well that is coming to you for advice.

Help them and expect nothing in return. Nothing. By helping them, you teach much more than the content of the conversation. You are indirectly teaching them a lesson of selflessness, service, and kindness.

This will be transferred to the people you help, and in turn, that quality will be brought to others.

I don't think Coach Boyle knew the impact he had on me. He was just being a great guy. Maybe this article, 10 years after the meeting, will help him understand.

I am very grateful to Coach Boyle for teaching me this lesson, and 10 years later, we still keep up a great relationship.

CHAPTER 11: ARE YOU WHO YOU WANT TO BE?

In this last chapter, I've put together some thoughts on being the person that you want to be. Are you grateful to those around you who serve on a daily basis? Do you listen to your kids? Are you getting stronger every day, in small, measurable ways? Read ahead for ideas on how to *never stop improving*.

Memorial Day

I originally recorded these thoughts on Memorial Day. Please read them and think of those serving our country.

The other day we had a man in our building who is in the Armed Services. He is training to be a combat medic and has trained with us for years. He came back to visit and had on his fatigues, dressed from head to toe in American pride.

One of our clients, who did not even know him, walked up to him and thanked him for his service. It struck me hard. I was not sure if I had ever done that. I thought about how much this great young man has sacrificed in his life, and the least we could do is thank him.

I thought about the mindset that these men and women need to display. I thought about SEALFIT and remembered that I had put myself on the line for only 12 hours and there was never a risk to my life.

This man will be doing things like that for years and may be in situations where his life in on the line. He deserves this. They all deserve our gratitude. I now make a point to thank the men and women in the Armed Forces for their services.

I am urging everyone to do the same. Say thank you to our service man and women if you see one. If there is a person you know in the Armed Forces and they are not around, write them a letter or a card and show gratitude for their sacrifice.

I learned a great lesson that day. Appreciation and recognition.

To us, Memorial Day is a fun weekend, a day off, a parade, or just a big BBQ. But Memorial Day is a day of remembering the men and women who died while serving in the United States Armed Forces.

It is important we do not forget the great men and women who protect our ability to live the lives we live in this great country. I hope everyone has a great day and takes a moment to think about all the great men and women who gave their lives for our ability to live our lives, free and safe.

To Sell is Human

I am going to recommend a tremendous book a few of us just finished reading called *To Sell Is Human: The Surprising Truth about Moving Others*, by Daniel H. Pink.

Many of you may be thinking that I am not in sales, but almost all of us are.

If you are mom, you are in sales. You are trying to sell your children on doing their homework, cleaning their room, and accomplishing other tasks. You are in sales.

One of the qualities they talked about was called buoyancy.

Buoyancy is being able to stay afloat in the midst of rejection. I write about this because of its similarity to the Growth Mindset.

With the Growth Mindset, rejection and failure are not dwelled upon or allowed to become destructive. They used this great exercise.

When something bad occurs, ask yourself these three questions and tell yourself NO.

- Is this Permanent?
- Is this Pervasive?
- Is this Personal?

The more likely you are to explain bad events as temporary, specific, and external, the more likely you are to persist in the face of adversity.

The third one really stood out to me, since I have read about this before in another book called *The Four Agreements: A Practical Guide to Personal Freedom*, by Don Miguel Ruiz. The ability to not take things personally is something that can truly help us live better lives.

If every occurrence with our spouse, children, friends, or co-workers is taken as a personal attack on our own self-worth, our thought process is affected, our happiness is compromised, and our thoughts and actions towards others do not represent who we truly are.

I believe not taking things personally is a skill that can be improved.

So the next time something negative happens to you truly ask yourself:

Is this Personal?

Tell yourself NO and move forward toward a happier, more successful life.

Praise for effort

I talked about this subject in an earlier section of the book, but I think it bears addressing again from a slightly different perspective.

By this time, I hope you have picked up a copy of *Mindset* by Carol Dweck; if not, get the book summary. I can assure you it is worth your time.

Most of us who deal with children—parents, coaches, teachers, and others—can sometimes get bogged down in the end result of sports or education: what kind of grades did they bring home, how many points did they score, what was the record?

Not to say that these things do not have any importance, but the tendency is to focus on rewarding for talent or intelligence such as an A on a test or scoring 25 points in a basketball game.

As parents, we are always trying to set our kids up for success. Well, I am here to report there is more effective way to praise your children that will spark the Growth Mindset.

The key is to praise your children for their effort. This encourages the Growth Mindset.

This concept should be on your mind when praising your kids, and it will take effort to keep reminding yourself to do this. An example could be, "I saw you got an A on that test. I am really proud of you for the effort you put in to earn that! Keep up the great work."

The following is a summary of Dweck's research on praising children:

"Educators commonly believe that praising students' intelligence builds their confidence and motivation to learn and that students' inherent intelligence is the major cause of their school achievement.

[Carol Dweck's] research shows that, on the contrary, praising students' intelligence can be problematic. Praise is intricately connected to how students view their intelligence.

Some students assume that intellectual ability is a fixed trait that either they have it or they don't. Students in this fixed mind-set seek tasks that prove their intelligence and avoid ones that they might struggle with.

Praising students for their intelligence tends to promote the fixed mind-set. Other students believe that they can develop their intellectual ability through effort and education. They take on challenges and learn from them.

Praising students for their effort encourages this growth mind-set. Interventions that make students aware of the plasticity of the brain and the malleable quality of intelligence motivate students by boosting their confidence in their ability to grow and learn."

So go ahead and praise away, but praise for EFFORT, not the end result.

Shut up and listen

Just about every day, I have a conversation with a parent about his or her children. It's one of my favorite parts of my job. I wish I was able to give better advice.

Many times it's hearing about how great they are doing, but a LOT of times I find myself having conversations about how their kids are struggling—struggling with sports, school, friends, injuries, etc.

I am not an expert on parenting.

I only have two young children whose biggest problems are a poopie diaper or a tantrum because her sister took her doll. I am by no means father of the year material. Yet, I still find myself in these conversations, most of time doing none of the talking.

In most cases, people are not looking for advice from me; they are looking for an ear, which I gladly lend because I know giving my ear has just as much impact, if not more, than giving advice.

I am in no way equipped to give parenting advice for a teen, but I can listen and I can empathize. This usually helps people feel much better about the situation. When directly asked for advice from a parent, the only real guidance I ever give is to do exactly what I did for them …

Listen.

This skill applies to parenting, leadership, coaching, marriages—anything where communication in involved. The better we listen, the better we communicate and the stronger our relationships will be.

I love this quote: God gave us two ears and one mouth for a reason.

So listen more and talk less. Ask more questions. Take note in your conversations throughout the week.

Do you find yourself dominating conversations, lecturing without asking questions? If so, it may be harder to develop a connection, or a deeper connection, with whom you are speaking.

A solid book to help with this is *Just Listen: Discover the Secret to Getting Through to Absolutely Anyone*, by Mark Goulston. He goes deeper with how the brain works and how people think, which will help us make more of an impact on others

Give listening more a shot. I am pretty sure relationships will strengthen and you will have more productive conversations.

Why do kids lie?

Attention, parents! Please share this section with your athletes.

From time to time, I become very disappointed with some of our athletes. We strive every day to bring out the best in our athletes and teach them about integrity, hard work, character, and honesty. I know that parents strive to do the same.

Many display this on a daily basis, but there have been more situations lately of athletes that simply lied to the faces of the GFP coaches, have been caught, and proceeded into a bigger lie. This has deeply disappointed us as coaches.

The only thing we have in this world is our word. Your word is an honest display of what you did or will do. It should be rock solid.

It does not matter whether it is about a food journal, something you did wrong, or a mistake you made—being honest with yourself, your parents, your coaches, and all others who try to help you succeed is imperative.

Your word is something that should be sacred to you. Not being honest about small things is the root of the Fixed Mindset.

If you forget your food journal and you make up excuses that get you deeper into a lie than before, it means you are afraid that the coach will think less of you as a person or that others in group will think less of you.

Forgetting your food journal will definitely not make us think less of you. It will simply provide us with another coaching opportunity as to why it is important for your success to bring in your food journal. This is one of the main reasons we do this exercise in the first place.

If you lie and then get away with it, what did you learn?

Nothing except how to be a better liar.

Is this what you want? To be a better liar that cannot be trusted?

Be impeccable with your word. Maybe it means you have to be embarrassed in front of your group if you forget your food journal. Maybe it means your group will have a little extra work at the end. Whatever the consequence, be impeccable with your word no matter what the issue is.

The reason is that lying about small things makes it easier to lie about bigger things. This is not the person you want to be. This is not who your parents want you to be, and it's certainly not who the GFP coaches want you to be.

Are you a person that says you will do something and then not do it?

Are you a person that just tells people what they want to hear?

Do you lie to people on a regular basis?

This needs to change right now because the only thing we have is our word. Step up, be a person of character, and be a person whom everyone in your life can be sure is being truthful and honest.

Preparation

After I originally wrote the preceding section about lying, I got a ton of feedback. Parents and even kids were coming up to me telling me they had read it. I am glad it hit home to many people because it is an important issue that should not be taken lightly.

This made me think about preparation. When you get caught in a lie, many times it is because you forget something you were supposed to bring, did not study, or simply forgot. Lack of preparation is one of those things that can bring out a person we are not.

If you fail a test, most likely it is not because you worked so hard and spent weeks preparing and just failed. It is because you did not take the steps to fully prepare yourself to succeed on the test.

I know you have all heard the saying, "Failing to prepare is preparing to fail." Many times prioritizing our time is a big reason why we may not achieve what we want. I know this because it is a personal weakness of mine and I spend a ton of time reading and learning how to improve my time management.

Not prioritizing our time is setting us up to be unprepared.

It is very easy for a high school student to plan his or her day. There are many hours where things are already planned, such as classes, practices, training, games, and so on, so simply filling in the rest is not that hard.

Studying, reading, extra training and practice, SAT prep, college work, or other tasks all must be planned out in advance in order to make sure they get done. I recommend keeping a calendar and planning each day the night before. It is important to know what is on the horizon to make sure time is dedicated to that. I use Google Calendar for this exercise.

Here's an example of a daily plan:

- 6 a.m. Wake up and get ready for school
- 6:30 Breakfast
- 7-7:30 Read
- 7:30-8:00 Get to school
- 8-2:30 p.m. School
- 3-5 Sports practice or off-season training
- 5:30-6:30 Homework and studying
- 6:30 Family and meal time
- 7:30 Homework/studying/reading/free time
- 10 p.m. Bed!

If students look at this calendar each day, they will have an idea of what is on the horizon. This makes being unprepared much less of a possibility. Of course, you will have a lot more details, like specific tests to study for or maybe tutoring sessions, extracurricular activities, and so forth.

So will taking a more proactive approach and prepare their day totally eliminate lying? I am not sure but it definitely cannot hurt.

Parents, how do you prioritize your time? Do you set a good example for your children to follow?

If not, start doing this yourself and then help your children develop this skill at an early age.

Prepare!

Basketball

I remember spending the entire recess period shooting baskets by myself.

I remember the ball I used, which basket it was at Salt Brook School, and what basket the other kids were playing at. It is as clear to me as it was 25 years ago.

I had been asked by everyone not to play with them anymore. I was banned. I remember this very empty feeling of being by myself. I do not remember doing anything to bring this on, but there were kids that did not want me to play basketball with the group anymore.

I tried so hard not to look at the other boys playing but it was impossible. I wanted to be included in the group. I kept on playing by myself for several weeks. I wish someone would have come and shot around with me. I wish someone could have stepped up and noticed I was upset about not being able to play with the group, but no one came.

I hear stories like this all the time from parents and kids, and I would love to find a way to prevent these situations. I am not sure it is possible, but the one thing we can do is strive to change the mindset of our youth.

We as parents need to teach our children that what others may think, say, or do to us does not define who we are, that if a few kids do not want to play basketball with us, it does not mean that we are inferior or will never play with other kids again. This does not mean it is not going to hurt our feelings, but if they decide not to take it personally, then it will not be viewed as "everyone has this view of me."

This is the Growth Mindset. This is a way of thinking.

The other thing to do is teach our children to always look out for others in trouble. To maybe not be concerned with what others will think about you if you go and play with the kid that no one wanted to play with.

There is a lot out there about bullying and situations that seem much more serious than this, but we never know how even the smallest situations will affect people. If just one person had come and played with me, I am pretty sure I would not even remember this.

Let's teach our kids to be aware of these situations and to step up and help others.

Self-discipline

Self-discipline is the ability to do what you should do, when you should do it, whether you feel like it or not.

The Growth Mindset teaches us that self-discipline is a skill and can be improved. It must be improved to achieve personal greatness in success in all aspects of our lives.

Think about your life and pick the thing that you are the most successful at. Do you lack discipline in that area? Most likely, NO. The main key to achieving personal greatness is self-discipline.

Many of us take the path of least resistance in our lives. We do what is easy now to avoid any pain or discomfort. Grabbing a bagel on your way to work is taking the path of least resistance toward your health. Yes, it is harder to cook your own breakfast before you leave the house, but we all know it's better in the long term for our bodies.

Short-term gain (getting a bagel) can cause long-term pain (poor health).

Self-discipline teaches us that it is OK to do what is hard and necessary rather than fun and easy. It puts us in a long-term thinking mindset. Most successful people have a long-term mindset.

The main message is that self-discipline is a skill. The more you practice it, the better you will get and the more success you will have in every aspect of your life.

How do get better at self-discipline? Educate yourself on self-discipline. Read a book about it, attend a seminar, ask someone with great self-discipline to teach you about it.

It is a skill.

The Growth Mindset tells us that we can improve our self-discipline in every area of our lives if we simply strive to get better at it.

Self-deception

I just finished reading a book called *Leadership and Self Deception: Getting Out of the Box*, from the Arbinger Institute. It was recommended to me by someone I respect, and they told me it has changed their life. When someone tells me a book has that kind of impact, I make time for it.

I recommend you read it, but I want to give you a little insight as to what I got out of it.

Self-deception is the problem of not being able to see that you are the problem.

When we are self-deceived we:

- Inflate others' faults
- Inflate our own virtue
- Blame others

Many times, we get so caught up in what we feel is right that we do not even consider the impact is has on others around us. We are unaware of our actions and decisions and do not even consider that they may have an adverse effect on others.

That is essentially the foundation of the message—to be able to see people as people and not objects. When you see people as people, you will consider how a specific situation will affect them as a person and not as an object that has no feelings or emotions.

This applies to every situation in our lives. It applies greatly to relationships.

After I read this book, I had Vanessa read it, and now we both have a better understanding of when we are inflating our own virtues and inflating the faults that we both have.

Every person in the world has faults, but in our relationships we must not define others by their faults but rather understand them and do not react or judge them.

Being free of self-deception creates an environment of openness, trust, and teamwork, where everyone acts for the collective good of the relationship, not their own virtues.

Now also understand that this is strongly related to mindset. I've discussed the fact that even when we are aware of the Fixed Mindset, we still can have it.

Self-deception is the same way. You may totally understand this concept and live your entire life around it, but we are human beings and we will have self-deception at some point. The key is to be aware of it and get back to treating people as people and not objects as fast as possible.

This concept applies to everything:

- Business
- Sports
- Marriage
- Relationships with your children
- Relationships with other family members
- Relationships with co-workers

Success and happiness for the long haul will be determined by being free of self-deception.

What does "GFP Strong" mean?

Around the gym, many of us wear sweatshirts that say "GFP Strong" on the front. We have gotten great feedback from them, and many clients have gotten one.

I wanted to clarify what GFP Strong really means and how it came about.

GFP Strong does not correlate with how much weight you lift. Although we want to see each of you get stronger in the gym, this is not the main definition of GFP Strong. Instead, it's our mindset that is what needs to be strong in all of us.

Without the Growth Mindset, all else is limited.

You are GFP strong if you live your life by these principles and give your best effort to set an example for your friends and family.

You are GFP Strong if you live all four aspects of the pyramid.

Doing so will provide a life full of health, happiness, and strength.

You are GFP Strong if you *have the Growth Mindset*.

- Treat failure as learning
- Always give your best effort
- Take criticism as feedback, not as a personal attack

You are GFP Strong if you *eat clean*.

- Eat whole foods
- Follow the 90 percent rule
- Be prepared

You are GFP Strong if you *train smart*.

- Move better, faster, stronger, longer
- Strive to improve every workout
- Be consistent

You are GFP Strong if you *recover*.

- Value sleep as essential
- Stretch or massage regularly
- De-stress through breathing

Are *you* GFP Strong?

CONCLUSION

I only ask one thing. I ask that you teach this Mindset to someone else. The only reason I was able to develop this mindset was because I taught it every week.

The best way to learn is to teach. Go spread this message. Be a positive light for others.

Be a Bumblebee.

Continue to add value and positivity to others—the store clerk, your mother in-law, your wife, your friend, your co-worker, someone just walking by.

In your time on this earth truly MAKE A DIFFERENCE.

ABOUT THE AUTHOR

Vince Gabriele is the owner of Gabriele Fitness & Performance, in Berkeley Heights, NJ. For the last 7 years this facility has become one of the most successful gyms on the east coast.

Vince has been featured in the Wall Street Journal, Web MD, Johnson and Johnson, the San Diego Union Tribune and has contributed articles and interviews for strengthcoach.com, elitefts.com, IYCA, strength coach TV and the stop chasing pain podcast.

Vince has a weekly blog called Mindset Monday that has run every week for 3 years.

Vince and his team now run business mentorships from their facility teaching trainers and business owners from around the country how to run their businesses more efficiently.

He is a regular speaker for many local universities, middle schools, sports teams and business seminars on various subjects including how to open your own facility, building a team, creating rock solid relationships and the growth mindset

Vince serves as a business consultant to over 20 fitness businesses across the US and Canada.

Vince played football at Temple University from 1998-2001 and then graduated from the University of San Diego with a degree in Business Administration in 2003. He received a masters degree in exercise science from California University of PA in 2007.

He is a graduate of the Goldman Sachs 10,000 small business.

To contact Vince Gabriele on his availability for business consulting and/or speaking engagements please send an e-mail to VINCE@GABRIELEFITNESS.COM and his assistant will follow up with you within 24-48 hours.